GU00372271

RR

Royal Society of

International Congress and Symposium Series

Editor-in-Chief: H. J. C. J. L'Etang

Number 92

The role of prostaglandins in labour

*Proceedings of a Symposium sponsored
by Upjohn Ltd, held in
London, 18 April, 1985*

Royal Society of Medicine Services Limited

International Congress and Symposium Series

Number 92

The role of
prostaglandins in labour

Edited by

CLIVE WOOD

1985

Published by

ROYAL SOCIETY OF MEDICINE SERVICES LIMITED
1 Wimpole Street, London W1M 8AE

ROYAL SOCIETY OF MEDICINE SERVICES LIMITED
1 Wimpole Street, London W1M 8AE

Distributed by
OXFORD UNIVERSITY PRESS
Walton Street, Oxford OX2 6DP
London   New York   Toronto
Delhi   Bombay   Calcutta   Madras   Karachi
Kuala Lumpur   Singapore   Hong Kong   Tokyo
Nairobi   Dar es Salaam   Cape Town
Melbourne   Auckland
and associated companies in
Beirut   Berlin   Ibadan   Mexico City   Nicosia
Oxford is a trade mark of Oxford University Press
   Copyright © 1985 by
ROYAL SOCIETY OF MEDICINE SERVICES LIMITED

These proceedings are published by Royal Society of Medicine Services Ltd with financial support from the sponsor. The contributors are responsible for the scientific content and for the views expressed, which are not necessarily those of the sponsor, of the editor of the series or of the volume, of the Royal Society of Medicine or of Royal Society of Medicine Services Ltd. Distribution has been in accordance with the wishes of the sponsor but a copy is available to any Fellow of the Society at a privileged price.

British Library Cataloguing in Publication Data
The role of prostaglandins in labour. —
   (International congress and symposium series,
   ISSN 0142-2367; no.92)
   1. Labor (Obstetrics)   2. Prostaglandins
   I. Wood, Clive
   II. Royal Society of Medicine   III. Series
   618.4   RG652

   ISBN 0-905958-19-5

Production services by Yvonne Rue, 45 New High Street, Oxford OX3 7AL
Phototypeset by Dobbie Typesetting Service, Plymouth, Devon
Printed in Great Britain at the University Press, Oxford

Contributors

Editor

C. Wood
Linacre College, Oxford, UK

Contributors

A. A. Calder
Department of Obstetrics and Gynaecology, Royal Infirmary, Glasgow, UK

A. Cameron
Department of Obstetrics and Gynaecology, Royal Infirmary, Glasgow, UK

J. Challis
Department of Obstetrics and Gynecology, St Joseph's Hospital, London, Ontario, Canada

A. P. Gordon-Wright
Redhill General Hospital, Earlswood Common, Redhill, Surrey, UK

H. Hinchley
Medical Adviser, Medical Services Division, Upjohn Limited, Fleming Way, Crawley, West Sussex, UK

P. Husslein
1 Universitäts Frauenklinik, Spitalgasse 23, 1090 Vienna 9, Austria

M. J. N. C. Keirse
Department of Obstetrics and Gynaecology, Leiden University Medical Centre, Rijnsburgerweg 10, 2333AA Leiden, Netherlands

W. L. Ledger
William Osler House, John Radcliffe Hospital, Headington, Oxford, UK

E. Lee
Department of Obstetrics and Gynaecology, St Mary's Maternity Hospital, Portsmouth, UK

I. Z. MacKenzie
Nuffield Department of Obstetrics and Gynaecology, John Radcliffe Hospital, Headington, Oxford, UK

M. McLaren
Department of Obstetrics and Gynaecology, Royal Infirmary, Glasgow, UK

A. Murray
Department of Obstetrics and Gynaecology, Arrowe Park Hospital, Wirral, Cheshire, UK

M. Read
Department of Obstetrics and Gynaecology, Withington Hospital, Manchester, UK

S. Sellers

Nuffield Department of Obstetrics and Gynaecology, John Radcliffe Hospital, Headington, Oxford, UK

P. Stewart

Northern General Hospital, Herries Road, Sheffield, South Yorkshire, UK

S. M. Walton

North Tees Hospital, Stockton-on-Tees, Cleveland, UK

Contents

Human labour — an interaction of muscle and gristle

A. A. CALDER

Department of Obstetrics and Gynaecology,
Royal Infirmary, Glasgow, UK

Parturition in the human being can be either easy or difficult. Sometimes difficulty arises because the foetus is too large or the mother's pelvis is too small, a complication seen at its most extreme among the rachitic dwarfs of last century. In the absence of such mechanical disparity, however, labour essentially consists of the overcoming by the uterus of the resistance offered by the soft tissues of the birth canal, notably the cervix. This relationship might usefully be described as an interaction of muscle and gristle.

The muscle, or myometrium, has preoccupied the attention of clinicians and investigators to the point where one grew almost to believe that it was the only thing that mattered. The onset of regular strong uterine contractions is, of course, the essence of parturition. However, there is much more to it than that, and almost 50 years ago W. H. Newton declared, 'Mere contraction of the uterus is too primitive a process to be dignified by the name of parturition'. More recently Liggins (1978) has added, 'Any hypothesis for the initiation of labour is incomplete unless it includes a satisfactory explanation for the structural changes in the cervix'.

William Hunter's dissection of the late pregnant uterus (Fig. 1) shows what has to be overcome for delivery to take place. The cervix, even at a late stage, is long and closed but it gradually shortens. Such a change can be seen in the cervix during the last few weeks of pregnancy and it is of interest to note that uterine contractility gradually builds up during this same phase, which has been called *pre-labour*.

Far from being a muscular structure, the cervix is predominantly composed of collagen (Danforth 1954). In the early pregnant state the collagen fibres are tightly packed, whereas in the postpartum condition they are widely separated and much more sparse. Thus both the muscle and the gristle in the uterus have to undergo profound changes for the process of parturition and it is these changes which form the basis of our discussions here today.

In the first session our attention will be concentrated on the physiological aspects of parturition, while in the second we will turn our attention to clinical considerations. In doing so, however, I hope that we will bear in mind the importance of a synchronous relationship between these two important biological functions in the corpus uteri and

The role of prostaglandins in labour, edited by Clive Wood, 1985: Royal Society of Medicine Services International Congress and Symposium Series No. 92, published by Royal Society of Medicine Services Limited.

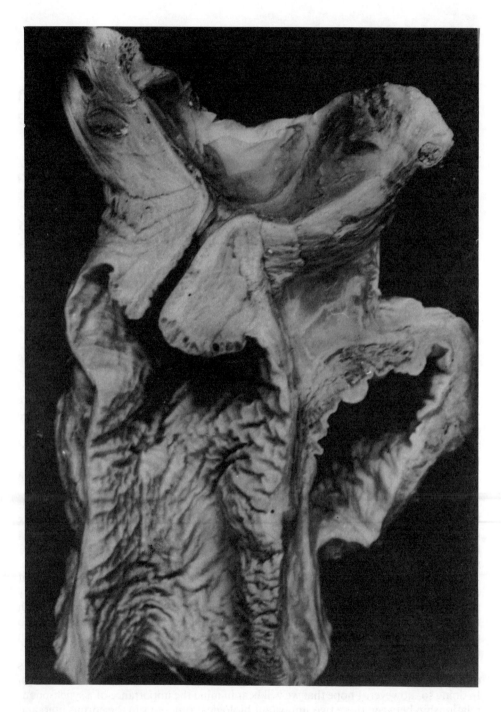

Figure 1. 'The cervix uteri in the ninth month of pregnancy' from a specimen prepared by William Hunter and described by him as 'a side view of the cervix uteri in its shut state, also of the vagina and bladder'. (From the Hunterian Anatomical Museum, Glasgow University, by kind permission of Professor R. J. Scothorne.)

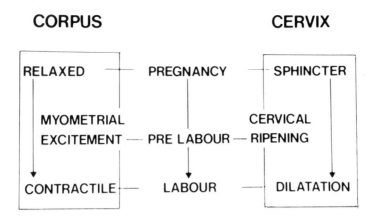

Figure 2. Schematic representation of the relationship between the corpus uteri and the cervix during pregnancy, pre-labour and labour.

in the cervix (Fig. 2). During pregnancy, the corpus must remain relaxed to allow the foetus to grow while the cervix must remain closed, rather like a sphincter. In labour these roles are changed, with the corpus becoming powerfully contractile and the cervix allowing itself to be fairly rapidly dilated. Normal parturition requires this change in roles. The changes take place gradually during pre-labour as the myometrium becomes more excitable and the cervix undergoes the process we know as *ripening*. And so we have to consider not only the endocrinology of myometrial contractility, a highly complicated matter and one in which our understanding has been rapidly advanced in recent years, but also the endocrinology of cervical ripening, which is perhaps less clearly understood but which has also been the subject of important advances.

Until recently oxytocin has been the cornerstone of clinical stimulation of myometrial contractility. We now recognize, however, that this agent — admirable though it may be in most circumstances — has a major deficiency in the difficult induction. If oxytocin is used to induce labour when the cervix is unripe the common finding is of prolonged labour, failure to progress and a high incidence of a need for caesarean section (Calder 1981). This is much more true of the primigravida than of the multigravida and it is the primigravida on whom our greatest concern must be focused.

Cervical dystocia has been the term applied to difficult labour due to a rigid, unyielding cervix and in days gone by some exotic techniques were applied to try to overcome it, not least the fearsome mechanical cervical dilators which were inserted into the cervix and then cranked open in an effort to achieve dilation. The success of such instruments is not recorded. More recently we recognized that while oxytocin stimulates good uterine contractions it has no beneficial effect on cervical ripening, whereas prostaglandins, notably prostaglandin E_2, appear to fulfil both requirements (Calder 1979). In summary then, when uterine contractility is seen in association with cervical ripening parturition is likely to follow the normal pattern, whereas if uterine contractility is generated in the absence of cervical ripening the outcome is likely to be dystocia.

Our subject today is prostaglandins and their role in the initiation of parturition. But I think perhaps we should address the rather broader remit of prostaglandins in parturition as a whole, since clearly they are involved not just in initiating this process but in seeing it through to its successful completion.

References

Calder, A. A. (1979). Management of the unripe cervix. In: *Human parturition*. Eds M. J. N. C. Keirse *et al.* Leiden University Press, Leiden, p. 201.

Calder, A. A. (1981). The human cervix in pregnancy and labour. In: *The cervix in pregnancy and labour*. Eds D. A. Elwood and A. B. M. Anderson. Churchill Livingstone, Edinburgh, p. 103.

Danforth, D. N. (1954). The distribution and functional activity of the cervical musculature. *American Journal of Obstetrics and Gynaecology* **68**, 1261.

Liggins, G. C. (1978). Ripening the cervix. *Seminars in Perinatology* **2**, 261.

Factors responsible for parturition

JOHN R. G. CHALLIS

*Department of Obstetrics and Gynecology
and Department of Physiology, University of Western Ontario,
St Joseph's Hospital Research Institute, London, Ontario, Canada*

Preterm labour remains a major problem in obstetrics and gynaecology. In our own hospital, which is a Level 3 referral centre for Southwestern Ontario, approximately 6·8 per cent of all deliveries are preterm. A variety of factors may predispose to preterm labour. These include socioeconomic factors, lifestyle and work habits, and medical factors associated with the current pregnancy, especially multiple gestation (Creasy, 1980). However, there remains a substantial proportion of patients presenting in idiopathic preterm labour. A major purpose in trying to understand the endocrine and physiological basis for labour is the hope of discovering why preterm delivery occurs in this group of idiopathic premature deliveries, and to explain in biochemical terms how predisposing, epidemiological components contribute to this condition.

Parturition is generally the consequence of a complex interplay of foetal and maternal factors. One may regard the onset of labour as resulting from sequential maturation of a series of organ systems. The sequence may begin at the level of the foetal brain or hypothalamus, and is transmitted through the pituitary to the foetal adrenal gland where, in animal models such as the sheep, cortisol provides the foetal trigger to the subsequent evolution of maternal endocrine changes (Thorburn and Challis 1979). These are reflected in the output of steroid hormones and prostaglandins from the placenta, the decidua and the foetal membranes and lead to increased stimulus to the myometrium, the responsiveness of which to potential agonists rises during late gestation. Cervical changes accompany the pattern of myometrial contractility which eventuates in birth. This review will consider the different steps on this sequential pathway, concentrating particularly on the production of prostaglandins and steroid hormones by intrauterine tissues the amnion, chorion and decidua.

Animal models

In animal models such as the sheep it is well established that the foetus, through increased activity of its pituitary–adrenal axis and increased cortisol output from the

The role of prostaglandins in labour, edited by Clive Wood, 1985: Royal Society of Medicine Services International Congress and Symposium Series No. 92, published by Royal Society of Medicine Services Limited.

foetal adrenal gland in late gestation, provides the signal for the onset of birth (Thorburn and Challis 1979). Hypophysectomy of the foetal lamb *in utero* obliterates the normal prepartum increase in foetal adrenal weight and rise in plasma cortisol concentrations, resulting in prolongation of gestation (Liggins *et al.* 1973). On the other hand, infusion of adrenocorticotrophic hormone (ACTH) to foetal sheep *in utero* results in a precocious increase in foetal adrenal weights, plasma cortisol concentrations, and premature delivery which, endocrinologically, may resemble the sequence of events seen at full term (Liggins 1973, Thorburn and Challis 1979). Recent work has shown that during late gestation in the sheep foetus there is an increase in the responsiveness of the foetal pituitary gland to secrete ACTH following stimulation by corticotrophic-releasing factor (Norman *et al.* 1985). This change is followed by an increase in responsiveness of the adrenal gland to secrete cortisol in response to ACTH stimulation. ACTH itself increases the steroidogenic machinery of the gland, including effects on adenylate cyclase activity and on a number of critical enzymes on the pathway to cortisol production (Challis *et al.* 1984). It is now evident that cortisol itself may play a role in modulating the mechanism by which ACTH activates foetal adrenal function (Challis *et al.* 1985a).

In sheep the rise in cortisol produces changes in placental steroidogenesis resulting in a decrease in the output of progesterone from the placenta into the maternal circulation, and a later increase in the concentration of unconjugated oestrogen. These changes in steroid hormones are followed by an increase in the concentration of prostaglandins (PG) in maternal and foetal plasma (Thorburn and Challis 1979). Using an animal model in which premature labour is provoked by infusing ACTH into the foetus in a pulsatile fashion, we have shown that the changes in prostaglandin concentration in amniotic fluid and maternal plasma are associated with an increase in the prostaglandin synthesizing activity of the intrauterine tissues, particularly the amnion and chorion, and precede that pattern of myometrial contractility that is characteristic of labour (Challis *et al.* 1985b).

Human studies

Attempts to apply the animal model directly to our understanding of human labour have been thwarted by an inability to demonstrate significant decreases in maternal peripheral plasma progesterone concentrations prior to birth. For this reason a number of investigators have sought changes in the production of steroid hormones and prostaglandins which may occur locally within the decidua and foetal membranes. Such changes might provide a signal for the onset of birth without being reflected in peripheral plasma hormone concentrations.

We have developed a model which suggests that the amnion and decidua are major sites of increasing prostaglandin production at the time of spontaneous labour in women. The chorion also produces prostaglandins, but has a much higher capacity to metabolize these compounds (Bleasdale and Johnston 1984). We have found that chorion and decidua also have a substantial capacity to produce steroid hormones, such as progesterone and oestrogens from appropriate substrates. We have discussed the possibility that one mechanism of regulating prostaglandin output from the foetal membranes may be through the local (paracrine or autocrine) effects of steroids produced within these same structures (Challis *et al.* 1985b). It is evident that the role of the foetus, and especially the foetal pituitary-adrenal axis, in human labour is less important than in animal models. However, as will be discussed later, factors of foetal origin reaching the foetal membranes through the amniotic fluid may also influence prostaglandin output by these structures. Of course, the membranes themselves are trophoblastic in origin.

Three major lines of evidence support a role for prostaglandins in the onset of labour (Thorburn and Challis 1979, Bleasdale and Johnston 1984)[1] There is an increase in the concentration of these compounds (PGE, PGF) in amniotic fluid, and of their metabolites in maternal plasma and urine in late pregnancy[2] Administration of drugs such as aspirin and indomethacin which are prostaglandin cyclo-oxygenase inhibitors suppress uterine activity and prolong the length of pregnancy. Further, the primate myometrium is exquisitely [3]sensitive to the stimulatory effects of exogenously administered prostaglandins.

Two additional important observations, which bear on the controls of prostanoid output, have also been made. First, the rise in prostaglandin concentrations in amniotic fluid at the time of labour is accompanied by an increase in the concentration of free arachidonic acid (Bleasdale and Johnston 1984) suggesting that liberation of this substrate may be critical for prostanoid production. Further, the rises in concentration of stimulatory prostaglandins (PGE and PGF) in amniotic fluid contrast with the relatively unimpressive changes in the concentrations of 6-keto $PGF_{1\alpha}$, the hydrolytic breakdown product of prostacyclin or PGI_2. This latter observation is of interest, since it may reflect directed endoperoxide metabolism towards stimulatory prostaglandins, and away from PGI_2 which, in women and in sheep, may have inhibitory actions on myometrial contractility (Lye and Challis 1982).

Various techniques have been used to study the probable sources of prostaglandins at term. We have shown, using dispersed cells from amnion, chorion, decidua and placenta, that the rate of PGE and PGF production per cell from amniotic and decidual tissue is higher when that tissue is collected from patients following spontaneous vaginal delivery, compared to the tissue from patients collected at elective caesarean section, at term, but in the absence of established labour (Skinner and Challis 1985). It is generally accepted that amnion is the major site of increased prostaglandin production at the time of labour (Okazaki *et al.* 1981, Bleasdale and Johnston 1984, Skinner and Challis 1985). The principle prostanoid produced by amnion is PGE, whereas decidua produces comparable amounts of PGE and PGF. In chorion cells, there was an increase in the output of 13,14-dihydro-15-keto $PGF_{2\alpha}$ (PGFM) in tissue taken from patients following spontaneous labour, which was not reflected in changed production of the primary prostaglandins. This observation substantiates earlier reports that the primary activity of chorion is prostaglandin metabolism, through high activities of the 15-dehydrogenase and reductase enzyme systems (Okazaki *et al.* 1981).

Prostaglandin production

A variety of factors which may influence prostaglandin production by foetal membranes have been delineated and studied extensively. The initial step in the formation of prostaglandins is the release of arachidonic acid from its esterified form in membrane phospholipids, principally phosphatidylethanolamine and phosphatidylinositol in amnion (Bleasdale and Johnston 1984). To release arachidonate, phosphatidylethanolamine requires the activity of a phospholipase A_2 enzyme, while phosphatidylinositol is a substrate initially of a phospholipase C enzyme, leading to the formation of arachidonate-rich diacylglycerol. This in turn is a substrate for further metabolism through diacylglycerol lipase and monoacylglycerol lipase to form arachidonic acid. It has been known for several years that there is a specific significant decrease in the amount of arachidonic acid, expressed as a percentage of total fatty acids, in phosphatidylinositol obtained from amnion during early labour, in comparison to values obtained before labour (Bleasdale and Johnston 1984). This result is compatible with increased mobilization of arachidonic acid from these phospholipid stores at the time of labour.

The availability of free calcium is a major factor influencing prostaglandin output by foetal membranes (Bleasdale *et al.* 1983, Bleasdale and Johnston 1984). It has been suggested that the probable mode of calcium action is through stimulation of phospholipases A_2 and C, and through inhibition of the enzyme diacylglycerol kinase, thereby preventing the re-synthesis of phosphatidylinositol. However, others have argued that the changes in calcium likely to occur *in vivo* are unlikely to be of sufficient magnitude to influence phospholipase activity, and indeed the specific activity of neither of the phospholipases increases with the onset of labour in humans (Okazaki *et al.* 1981). It is possible that calcium effects may be on other enzymes, or on a protein kinase which may phosphorylate, and thereby inactivate, the macromolecular protein lipomodulin which, in other systems, inhibits phospholipase activity (Bleasdale *et al.* 1983).

Work in our laboratory has shown that removal of extracellular calcium from the medium bathing amnion cells *in vitro*, or blocking calcium entry into those cells with D-600 (verapamil) attenuates PGE_2 output (Olson *et al.* 1983a). Conversely, if the intracellular calcium concentration is increased by addition of the calcium ionophore A23187 to the extracellular medium, there is a 2- to 3-fold increase in prostaglandin output. It is possible that the effects of calcium on prostaglandin production may be mediated by intracellular calcium-binding proteins. We have found that the stimulatory effect of A23187 on prostaglandin output by amnion and decidual tissue is inhibited, in a dose-dependent fashion, by the calmodulin antagonist trifluoperazine (TFP) with an IC_{50} of around 10 μm TFP (Warwick *et al.* 1985). Olson *et al.* (1985) have shown that calmodulin-like activity is present in both the cytosolic and microsomal portions of the amnion. This activity promotes phosphodiesterase hydrolysis of cAMP, and is calcium-dependent. At the present time the site of calcium-calmodulin interaction in prostaglandin production is unclear.

A variety of activities have been found in amniotic fluid which may inhibit or stimulate prostaglandin production. Mitchell and colleagues have shown that the activity known as endogenous inhibitor of prostaglandin synthesis (EIPS), found in maternal and foetal plasma and amniotic fluid, decreases in amniotic fluid with the onset of labour (Saeed *et al.* 1982). Its actions have been demonstrated in bovine seminal vesicle preparations. This activity appears to affect PG synthesis at the level of the cyclo-oxygenase enzyme. Casey and colleagues (1983) have recently described an activity in samples of newborn (foetal) urine which stimulates by several-fold the output of PGE_2 from human amnion cells maintained in monolayer tissue culture. This activity is also present in amniotic fluid in late gestation. Its effects on amnion cells are time- and protein-dependent, and are specific. Myometrial cells, endometrial tissue or adipose tissue maintained in monolayer culture, failed to respond with enhanced PG production to this material. The effects of human foetal urine on the output of PGE_2 by amnion cells are similar to those obtained during incubation with epidermal growth factor (EGF), and amnion cells are known to contain EGF receptors. At the present time, however, it appears that the stimulatory component of foetal urine is not EGF *per se*, but may be a related or derived growth factor.

Other workers have reported macromolecular components of amnion and of decidual cytosol which influence PG production *in vitro* although the *in vivo* significance of these components is unclear at present.

Di Renzo *et al.* (1984) have recently shown that amnion cells possess β-receptors, predominantly of the β_2 subtype. It has been suggested that this tissue may respond to the rising concentrations of catecholamines that are present in amniotic fluid during late gestation, perhaps as a reflection of foetal adrenal medullary maturation (Divers *et al.* 1981). Both amnion and decidua contain active adenylate cyclase systems, which can be stimulated with β-agonists such as isoproteronol, PGE_1, forskolin and cholera toxin (Di Renzo *et al.* 1984, Warrick *et al.* 1985). The effects of forskolin and cholera toxin on cyclic AMP output by amniotic and decidual cells were temporarily associated with an increase in the output of prostaglandins by these tissues. The effects of activators of adenylate cyclase on PG biosynthesis could be mimicked by addition of dibutyryl cAMP or phosphodiesterase inhibitors such as methylxanthine (MIX) to the cells in incubation (Warrick *et al.* 1985). The effects of MIX and A23187 in stimulating PG output by amniotic cells were partially additive. Further, dbcAMP-stimulated PG output by amniotic and decidual cells was attenuated by TFP in a dose-dependent fashion, resembling the effect of this calmodulin antagonist on prostaglandin production stimulated by A23187. These experiments suggest that β-agonists may stimulate PGE and PGF output by amniotic and by decidual cells. The effects depend on at least a basal availability of calcium to the cells and raise the possibility (see below) that both cyclic AMP-dependent and cyclic AMP-independent protein kinases may be important in relation to prostaglandin generation (Warrick *et al.* 1985).

These results are somewhat surprising because of the clinical use of β-sympatho-mimetic drugs in the management of preterm labour. However, it should be realized that PGI_2, an inhibitory prostaglandin, has not yet been measured in these types of studies, nor has the effect of β-agonists on myometrial production of prostaglandins *per se* yet been studied.

Johnston and colleagues (Billah and Johnston 1983, Bleasdale and Johnston 1984) have recently reported that platelet activating factor (1-O-alkyl-2-acetyl-3-glycerophosphocholine) is present in amniotic fluid at term and in term foetal membranes, and that the amnion possesses the enzymes responsible for its synthesis and metabolism. Skinner and Challis (unpublished) and Bleasdale and Johnston (1984) have shown that addition of PAF to amniotic cells in culture or in incubation provokes a 2- to 3-fold increase in the output of prostaglandin E_2, the effect resembling that seen with A23187. In platelets, PAF stimulates inositol phospholipid turnover and increases the availability of diacylglycerol. This compound is rich in arachidonic acid and its transient formation may be associated with activation of protein kinase C (Nishizuka 1984). In addition, inositol triphosphate (IP3) formed from phosphati-dylinositol-4-phosphate or phosphatidylinositol-4,5-biphosphate releases calcium from intracellular stores, most likely endoplasmic reticulum. Okazaki *et al.* (1984) have shown that protein kinase C activity is present in human foetal membranes. Olson (unpublished) has also shown that the phorbol ester (TPA) which stimulates protein kinase C activity, promotes PGE_2 synthesis in dispersed amniotic cell preparations.

The effects of steroid hormones on prostaglandin production by the human foetal membranes have been largely established by extrapolation from experiments with other tissues and in other species, rather than from direct experimentation. It is known that oestrogen stimulates and progesterone inhibits the output of $PGF_{2\alpha}$ from secretory endometrium obtained from non-pregnant women and maintained in tissue culture (Abel and Baird 1980). Progesterone blocked the stimulatory action of oestrogen on $PGF_{2\alpha}$ output by this tissue. Similar results have been obtained by Schatz and Gurpide (1983) who emphasized that the effect of oestradiol was primarily on the glandular cell epithelium isolated from the endometrium. We have found that oestrogen provokes a modest increase in the output of PGE_2 by decidual cell preparations obtained from patients at elective caesarean section (Olson *et al.* 1983b).

The stimulatory effect on PGE_2 output was associated with a reduction in the output of 6-keto $PGF_{1\alpha}$ by these same cell preparations. 6-keto $PGF_{1\alpha}$ output presumably reflects production of prostacyclin, an inhibitory prostaglandin (Lye and Challis 1982). We reasoned that oestrogen may affect endoperoxide metabolism, and hence the ratio of stimulatory to inhibitory prostaglandins produced by decidua, and perhaps by foetal membranes. To date, no direct effects of progesterone on prostaglandin production by the foetal membranes have been demonstrated. However, most investigators have sought only actions on basal prostanoid output, and more subtle effects, e.g. on phospholipid turnover, and on calcium-stimulated prostaglandin release, are only currently being examined.

The potential exists, however, for steroid hormones produced within the foetal membranes and decidua to modulate local prostaglandin production. We have found that chorion and decidua have high activities of the 3β-hydroxysteroid dehydrogenase enzyme, thereby converting pregnenolone to progesterone (Mitchell *et al.* 1982). In addition, these structures avidly convert oestrone sulphate to oestrone and to oestradiol (Mitchell *et al.* 1984). Oestrone sulphate is present in increasing concentrations in human amniotic fluid in late gestation and could readily pass to the membranes to serve as substrate for production of unconjugated oestrogen. In addition, potential substrates are present within the maternal circulation. We have found also that the activity of the oestrone sulphate sulphatase enzyme increases several-fold in tissue collected from patients following spontaneous delivery compared to the activity in tissue collected from patients at elective caesarean section (Mitchell *et al.* 1984). Oestrone and oestradiol exert a direct inhibitory effect on the conversion of pregnenolone to progesterone (Mitchell *et al.* 1982).

We have speculated therefore that oestrogen made locally within chorion and decidua could, within those same structures, shut off progesterone production and effect a substantial change in the oestrogen/progesterone ratio. Such a change could be one factor in affecting the balance between production of stimulatory and inhibitory prostaglandins within the foetal membranes and myometrium. In addition, an increase in oestrogen locally could account for the increase in the oxytocin receptor population in the myometrial cells (Alexandrova and Soloff 1980). In animals, oestrogen also increases uterine responsiveness to $PGF_{2\alpha}$. Garfield *et al.* (1980) have shown that an increase in the oestrogen/progesterone ratio is an important factor in increasing the number of gap junctions present between myometrial cells, thereby facilitating the spread of electrical conductivity within this muscle layer.

The control of myometrial activity *per se* has been described in several recent reviews (see Huszar and Naftolin 1984). Briefly, it depends upon the enzymatic phosphorylation of the myosin light chains to allow interaction with actin to form actomyosin. Myosin light chain kinase (MLCK) is a key enzyme in effecting this phosphorylation. Calcium, after binding to calmodulin, is essential for the activation of MLCK. Thus, agents that influence the availability of calcium affect MLCK activity and myometrial contractility. Within the myometrial cell, calcium levels are regulated by the intracellular calcium pool, by sequestration within storage vesicles (sarcoplasmic reticulum), and by fluxes of calcium across the cell membrane. Thse fluxes may be effected through calcium channels, or through the calcium-magnesium-dependent ATPase system. Oxytocin appears to stimulate myometrial activity by preventing extrusion of calcium through this latter system. Agents such as prostaglandins may promote release of calcium from intracellular pools, or prevent uptake of calcium into those pools. Agents such as progesterone and β-agonists, acting through cyclic AMP-dependent protein kinases, promote sequestration of calcium within the sarcoplasmic reticular pools.

MLCK activity is also influenced directly through phosphorylation by cAMP-dependent kinases, and thus by the intracellular cAMP concentration (Huszar and Naftolin 1984). In turn, the levels of cAMP within the cell reflect the balance between adenylate cyclase and phosphodiesterase activity. Beta-adrenergic stimulation, or β-sympathomimetic drugs such as terbutaline or isoproterenol, which stimulate adenylate cyclase, thus inhibit MLCK activity. On the other hand, agents such as theophylline or α-adrenergic effectors, which inhibit phosphodiesterase activity and prevent cAMP breakdown also elevate intracellular cAMP levels, with resultant activation of cAMP-dependent kinases. It is not clear at present whether the prostaglandins that influence myometrial contractility are generated directly within that structure, are produced in decidua, or are able to gain access to these structures from amnion. It has been argued that PGE produced in the amnion may escape metabolism in the chorion to reach the decidua, where it promotes further prostaglandin production and/or is converted in part to $PGF_{2\alpha}$ through the 9-keto reductase enzyme (Casey and MacDonald 1983). These prostanoids would then interact with prostaglandin receptors on myometrial cells in a paracrine fashion. In this context, prostaglandins may also function as calcium ionophores promoting uptake of extracellular calcium, in addition to any effects on the intracellular calcium pool (Huszar and Naftolin 1984).

Other agents known to affect myometrial contractility can be incorporated within this scheme. Relaxin, produced by the ovary in some species, and possibly by decidua, promotes uterine quiescence, perhaps through interacting with cell surface receptors, activating adenylate cyclase, and by increasing the intracellular cyclic AMP concentration (Sanborn *et al.* 1980). Alternately, it has recently been reported that relaxin stimulates production of PGI_2 (Richardson *et al.* 1984). It would be of interest to establish whether the effects of this peptide were dependent on mediation through prostanoid biosynthesis.

These observations provide a rationale for methods currently used to stop labour, and for the development of new methods to suppress myometrial contractility. Beta-mimetics act through cyclic AMP-dependent protein kinases to affect MLCK activity and calcium availability, although their contradictory stimulatory effect on PGE and PGF in amnion cells requires further explanation. Drugs which block prostaglandin production, or analogues of prostacyclin which may inhibit uterine activity, will be of continued interest. A new generation of calcium channel blockers may exert their action directly on the myometrium to reduce the availability of calcium necessary for MLCK activation. Alternatively, these drugs may exert other indirect effects on prostaglandin generation. At the present time, the biochemistry underlying the enhanced capacity for prostaglandin production by tissue obtained at spontaneous labour compared to that of elective caesarean section remains unresolved. The effects, if any, of steroids on prostaglandin production in human foetal membranes, decidua and myometrium at term, await rigorous experimental proof. Extrapolation of those observations to the patient in preterm labour is awaited. Finally, certainty that the patient is actually presenting in preterm labour remains a prerequisite in therapeutic trials and management strategies based on these underlying physiological mechanisms.

Acknowledgements

Work in the author's laboratory is supported by the Medical Research Council of Canada (MRC Group Grant in Reproductive Biology) and by the Physicians' Services Incorporated of Ontario (grant with Dr B. F. Mitchell). It is a pleasure to acknowledge the involvement of many colleagues, especially Drs D. M. Olson, S. J. Lye and B. F. Mitchell and Ms K. A. Skinner in the studies described in this review.

References

Abel, M. H. and Baird, D. T. (1980). The effect of 17β-estradiol and progesterone on prostaglandin production by human endometrium maintained in organ culture. *Endocrinology* **106**, 1599.

Alexandrova, M. and Soloff, M. S. (1980). Oxytocin receptors and parturition: 1. Control of oxytocin receptor concentrations in the rat myometrium at term. *Endocrinology* **106**, 730.

Billah, M. M. and Johnston, J. M. (1983). Identification of phospholipid platelet-activating factor (1-0-alkyl-2-acetyl-*sn*-glycero-3-phosphocholine) in human amniotic fluid and urine. *Biochemical and Biophysical Research Communications* **113**, 51.

Bleasdale, J. E., Okazaki, T., Sagawa, N., Di Renzo, G. C., Okita, J. R., MacDonald, P. C. and Johnston, J. M. (1983). The mobilization of arachidonic acid for prostaglandin production during parturition. In *Initiation of parturition: prevention of prematurity* (Eds P. C. MacDonald and J. Porter). Fourth Ross Conference on Obstetric Research, Ross Laboratories, Columbus, Ohio. p. 129.

Bleasdale, J. E. and Johnston, J. M. (1984). Prostaglandins and human parturition: regulation of arachidonic acid mobilization. *Review of Perinatal Medicine* **5**, 157.

Casey, M. L. and MacDonald, P. C. (1983). Pisseaktis in human amniotic fluid. Annual Meeting of the Endocrine Society, San Antonio, Texas (Abstract 600).

Casey, M. L., MacDonald, P. C. and Mitchell, M. D. (1983). Stimulation of prostaglandin E_2 production in amnion cells in culture by a substance(s) in human foetal and adult urine. *Biochemical and Biophysical Research Communications* **114**, 1056.

Challis, J. R. G., Mitchell, B. F. and Lye, S. J. (1984). Activation of fetal adrenal function. *Journal of Developmental Physiology* **6**, 93.

Challis, J. R. G., Hubtanen, D., Sprague, C., Mitchell, B. F. and Lye, S. J. (1985a). Modulation by cortisol of ACTH-induced activation of adrenal function in fetal sheep. *Endocrinology* (In press).

Challis, J. R. G., Lye, S. J., Mitchell, B. F., Olson, D. M., Sprague, C., Norman, L., Power, S. G. A., Siddiqi, J. and Wlodek, M. (1985b). Fetal signals for birth. *Journal of Developmental Physiology* (In press).

Creasy, R. K. (1980). Prevention of preterm labor. In *Premature labor*. Mead Johnson Symposium on Perinatal and Developmental Medicine, Vol. 15, p. 37.

Di Renzo, G. C., Venincasa, M. D. and Bleasdale, J. E. (1984). The identification and characterization of β-adrenergic receptors in human amnion tissue. *American Journal of Obstetrics and Gynecology* **148**, 398.

Divers, W. A., Wilkes, M. M., Babknia, A. and Yen, S. S. C. (1981). An increase in catecholamines and metabolites in the amniotic fluid compartment from middle to late gestation. *American Journal of Obstetrics and Gynecology* **139**, 483.

Garfield, R. E., Merrett, D. and Grover, A. K. (1980). Gap junction formation and regulation in myometrium. *American Journal of Physiology* **239**, C217.

Huszar, G. and Naftolin, F. (1984). The myometrium and uterine cervix in normal and preterm labor. *New England Journal of Medicine* **311**, 571.

Liggins, G. C., Fairclough, R. J., Grieves, S. A., Kendall, J. Z. and Knox, B. S. (1973). The mechanism of initiation of parturition in the ewe. *Recent Progress in Hormonal Research* **29**, 111.

Lye, S. J. and Challis, J. R. G. (1982). Inihibition by PGI-2 of myometrial activity *in vivo* in non-pregnant ovariectomized sheep. *Journal of Reproduction and Fertility* **66**, 311.

Mitchell, B. F., Cruikshank, B., McLean, D. and Challis, J. R. G. (1982). Local modulation of progesterone production in human foetal membranes. *Journal of Clinical and Endocrinological Metabolism* **55**, 1237.

Mitchell, B. F., Cross, J., Hobkirk, R. and Challis, J. R. G. (1984). Formation of unconjugated estrogens from estrone sulphate by dispersed cells from human fetal membranes and decidua. *Journal of Clinical and Endocrinological Metabolism* **58**, 845.

Nishizuka, Y. (1984). The role of protein kinase C in cell surface signal transduction and tumour promotion. *Nature (London)* **308**, 693.

Norman, L. J., Lye, S. J. and Challis, J. R. G. (1985). Changes in fetal ACTH responses to CRF during late gestation. *Canadian Journal of Physiology and Pharmacology* (In press).

Okazaki, T., Casey, M. L., Okita, J. R., MacDonald, P. C. and Johnston, J. M. (1981). Initiation of human parturition, XII. Biosynthesis and metabolism of prostaglandins in human fetal membranes and uterine decidua. *American Journal of Obstetrics and Gynecology* **139**, 373.

Okazaki, T., Ban, C. and Johnston, J. M. (1984). The identification and characterization of protein kinase C activity in fetal membranes. *Archives of Biochemistry and Biophysics* **229**, 27.

Olson, D. M., Opavsky, M. A. and Challis, J. R. G. (1983a). Prostaglandin synthesis by human amnion is dependent upon extracellular calcium. *Canadian Journal of Physiology and Pharmacology* **61**, 1809.

Olson, D. M., Skinner, K. and Challis, J. R. G. (1983b). Estradiol-17β and 2-hydroxyestradiol-17β-induced differential production of prostaglandins by cells dispersed from human intrauterine tissues at parturition. *Prostaglandins* **25**, 639.

Olson, D. M., Kramar, D. and Smieja, Z. (1985). Identification of calmodulin-like activity in human amnion. Possible role in prostaglandin biosynthesis. (Submitted for publication).

Richardson, M., Mitchell, M. D., MacDonald, P. C. and Casey, M. L. (1984). Effect of relaxin on prostacyclin production by human myometrial cells in monolayer culture. Society for Gynecological Investigation Annual Meeting, San Francisco, California (Abstract 402).

Saeed, S. A., Strickland, D. M., Young, D. C., Dang, A. and Mitchell, M. D. (1982). Inhibition of prostaglandin synthesis by human amniotic fluid. Acute reduction in inhibitory activity of amniotic fluid obtained during labor. *Journal of Clinical Endocrinology and Metabolism* **55**, 801.

Sanborn, B. M., Kuo, H. S., Weisbrodt, N. W. and Sherwood, O. D. (1980). The interaction of relaxin with the rat uterus. 1. Effect on cyclic nucleotide levels and spontaneous contractile activity. *Endocrinology* **106**, 1210.

Schatz, F. and Gurpide, E. (1983). Effects of estradiol on prostaglandin $F_{2\alpha}$ levels in primary monolayer cultures of epithelial cells from human proliferative endometrium. *Endocrinology* **113**, 1274.

Skinner, K. A. and Challis, J. R. G. (1985). Changes in the synthesis and metabolism of prostaglandins by human fetal membranes and decidua at labor. *American Journal of Obstetrics and Gynecology* **151**, 519.

Thorburn, G. D. and Challis, J. R. G. (1979). Endocrine control of parturition. *Physiological Reviews* **59**, 863.

Warrick, C., Skinner, K., Mitchell, B. F. and Challis, J. R. G. (1985). Relation between cyclic AMP and prostaglandin output by dispersed cells from human amnion and decidua. *American Journal of Obstetrics and Gynecology* (In press).

Discussion

Dr Keirse said that Dr Challis was assuming that prostacyclin had an inhibitory effect in the human myometrium in pregnancy. However, the data seemed to be based on findings in the non-pregnant sheep. The literature suggested that prostacyclin might exert a stimulatory or inhibitory effect but such findings had been obtained *in vitro*. He knew of no *in vivo* studies in human subjects.

Dr Challis said that *in vitro* data using human myometrial strips had shown inhibitory effects of prostacyclin. The effect was probably mediated through cAMP. The inhibitory effects that they had found in the sheep contrasted with the situation in the rat, where PGI_2 appeared to be stimulatory. It was not clear why the effect should depend on the species. The question could be resolved by administering PGI_2 to normal patients in late pregnancy, but such a study would create major ethical problems. Studies in which PGI_2 had been administered into the uterine lumen were difficult to interpret with respect to changes in myometrial activity because of the possible uterine metabolism of PGI_2. Conversion to 6-keto PGI_2, a single enzymatic step, would produce a compound that, at least in sheep, would stimulate myometrial activity.

PGI_2 had been given to a few patients with hypertension on the assumption that it would have a vasodilatory effect, and there were suggestions that it exerted a reduction in uterine activity, but such findings have never been reported in a large series of patients.

Dr Calder said that patients with severe pre-eclampsia reputedly had very low prostacyclin activity but their condition was not marked by excessive uterine contractility. He wondered whether in normal pregnancy there were large amounts of prostacyclin which disappeared prior to labour.

Dr Challis said that in most species that had been examined PGI_2 (measured as 6-keto $PGF_{1\alpha}$) was the major prostaglandin in the myometrium. In pre-eclamptic patients the amount of PGI_2 appeared to be reduced. Again, the question could only be resolved by examining samples of myometrium from late gestation. In the absence of such data, studies on lower primates might throw light on the question.

Mode of action of oxytocin and the role of its receptor in the production of prostaglandins

P. HUSSLEIN

First Clinic of Obstetrics and Gynaecology,
University of Vienna, Austria

The nonapeptide oxytocin is synthetized in the paraventricular and supraoptic nuclei of the hypothalamus, bound to its neurophysin and transported in neurosecretory granules into the posterior pituitary gland where these granules are stored until released by appropriate stimuli. These include mechanical stimulation of the nipples, cervical and vaginal dilatation (at least in animals—the *Ferguson reflex*) and possibly hormones like oestrogens, prostaglandins (PG) and thyrotropin-releasing hormones (Dawood 1983).

The secretion of oxytocin is episodic and has been described as a 'spurt release'. From observations of electrical activity of the hypothalamic nuclei it is known that oxytocin secreting neurons fire at random at intervals between 4 and 8 min. Whether plasma levels change in a similar fashion has been a matter of debate but current data make it rather unlikely.

Until recently, the importance of oxytocin for the initiation of labour had been generally well accepted. The following indirect evidence supported the assumption:

(1)   Oxytocin is by far the most potent and specific stimulus to the pregnant human uterus.

(2)   In certain animals, notably rabbits and rats, secretion of oxytocin is clearly associated with the initiation of labour.

(3)   At term, exogenous oxytocin is highly effective in inducing labour in women.

(4)   Anencephalic pregnancies with a deficiency of the posterior lobe of the pituitary are of clearly disordered length.

(5)   Ethanol, which is known to inhibit oxytocin release both in animals and women, has been successfully used to treat premature labour.

With the advent of radioimmunoassay (RIA; Chard *et al.* 1970) more detailed investigations became possible. The lack of measurable levels of oxytocin during human labour in some studies (Chard *et al.* 1970) and the wide range of oxytocin levels during pregnancy and labour in others (Gibbens *et al.* 1972; Kumaresan *et al.* 1975; Dawood *et al.* 1978; Leake *et al.* 1981) caused the role of oxytocin in the

The role of prostaglandins in labour, edited by Clive Wood, 1985: Royal Society of Medicine Services
International Congress and Symposium Series No. 92, published by Royal Society of Medicine Services
Limited.

initiation of labour to become heavily disputed. The main argument against an involvement of oxytocin in the initiation of parturition has been a lack of any demonstrable increase in oxytocin plasma levels before parturition or in very early labour (Sellers *et al.* 1981).

However, it is well known from clinical experience that the sensitivity of the myometrium towards oxytocin changes dramatically during pregnancy, though different opinions have been expressed as to whether this increase takes place during the third trimester or shortly before term (Caldeyro-Barcia and Sereno 1961). In order to evaluate the responsiveness of the myometrium to oxytocin we developed an *oxytocin sensitivity test*. A small fixed dose of oxytocin (10 mIU) is administered 3 times during an interval of 1 min and uterine contractions are monitored before and after the injection by means of external tocography. A scoring system was devised as follows:

(1) If no contractions could be observed after 3 injections the test was considered negative (0 points).

(2) If 1–2 contractions could be observed, or if contractions were felt by the patients but could not be demonstrated on the tocogram, the test result was evaluated as intermediate (1 point).

(3) If regular contractions were induced, a high oxytocin sensitivity was assumed and the test was considered positive (2 points; Fig. 1).

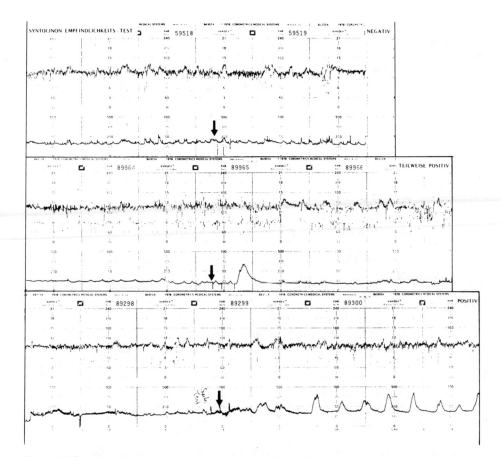

Figure 1. Scoring of the oxytocin sensitivity test. Negative results (top); intermediate result (centre); positive result (bottom). Oxytocin injected at arrow.

Clinical studies

We recruited a group of 26 healthy pregnant women in whom the length of pregnancy was established by accurate dates and early ultrasound measurements. Oxytocin sensitivity, cervical score and the plasma concentrations of oxytocin and of 13,14-dihydro-15-keto prostaglandin $F_{2\alpha}$ (PGFM), were determined on a daily basis until the onset of spontaneous labour. Fig. 2 summarizes the results. As expected from data in the literature, the oxytocin plasma concentration did not change in the last week before spontaneous labour, whereas the mean oxytocin sensitivity increased dramatically during the same period. Seven days before the onset of labour none of the patients showed maximal oxytocin sensitivity, with 50 per cent of them having a completely negative test, whereas on the day of spontaneous onset of contractions almost all of them were maximally oxytocin sensitive. PGFM levels remained unchanged during this period, whereas the mean cervical score increased markedly (Kofler *et al.* 1983).

Following these clinical results, indicating a marked rise in the myometrial responsiveness to oxytocin, it seemed appropriate to examine the biochemical

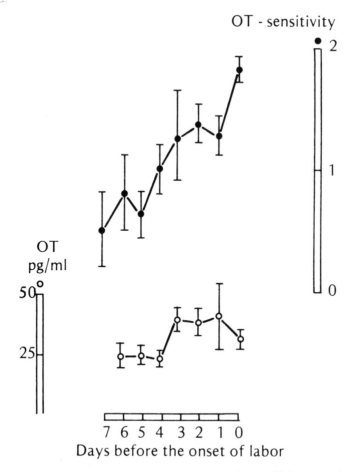

Figure 2. Oxytocin sensitivity determined by the oxytocin sensitivity test related to plasma levels of oxytocin during the last days before the onset of spontaneous labour.

Table 1

Oxytocin receptors in the myometrium of human uteri
All values mean ± SE (fmol/mg DNA)

Condition	n	Receptor concentration
Nonpregnant, menstruating	14	27·6± 7·97
Pregnant (13–17 weeks)	5	171·6± 67·4
Preterm labour (28–36 weeks)	8	2353 ±358
Before labour (37–43 weeks)	6	1391 ±180
Early labour (37–43 weeks)	5	3468 ±886

mechanism for this increase in sensitivity. To investigate whether binding sites for oxytocin do in fact mediate its action on the uterus, specific binding site concentrations were first measured in pregnant rats (Fuchs *et al.* 1983). An excellent correlation between the oxytocin receptor concentration and the uterine response to exogenous oxytocin was found, providing strong support for the assumption that the specific binding sites do indeed represent the physiological receptors for oxytocin.

We subsequently compared the oxytocin receptor concentration in non-pregnant controls with that in pregnant women at different stages of gestation (Fuchs *et al.* 1982, Fuchs *et al.* 1984). Samples were obtained at hysterectomy, hysterotomy in the second trimester and caesarean section in the third trimester and at term. Table 1 shows a 10-fold increase in oxytocin receptor concentration during pregnancy, with significantly higher levels in early labour compared to term gestation with no contractions (Sakamoto *et al.* 1979, Fuchs *et al.* 1982, Fuchs *et al.* 1984). These findings appear to provide a biochemical explanation for the increased myometrial responsiveness to oxytocin at term and to the rise in sensitivity shown beforehand.

From these results it is clear that when oxytocin sensitivity increases because of a rise in oxytocin receptors in the myometrium, the oxytocin concentration necessary

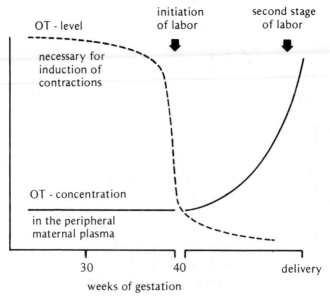

Figure 3. Hypothetical scheme relating the fall in oxytocin (OT) threshold to the rise in OT sensitivity.

to achieve the threshold level required to induce uterine contractions must necessarily fall. Thus, the argument that oxytocin cannot trigger the onset of labour because its peripheral plasma concentration does not rise beforehand is clearly untenable (Fig. 3)

One difficulty, however, remained. Labour has definitely been shown to be associated with a rise of PG levels, mainly PGFM. If a link between the increase in oxytocin activity at term and the rise in PG levels could be demonstrated, evidence for the role of oxytocin would be further reinforced.

Tissue studies

When the oxytocin receptor content of samples of decidua parietalis was measured we found, to our surprise, that decidua also contains a significant number of oxytocin binding sites (Fuchs *et al.* 1981). As in the case of the myometrium, the concentration of decidual oxytocin receptors was relatively low in mid pregnancy, rising to maximum values in uteri from patients in term labour. The concentrations in decidua parietalis were generally similar to those of the myometrium. Comparison of the dissociation constants showed that the affinity for oxytocin was unchanged throughout gestation and that this was indistinguishable from that of myometrial samples.

As a result of these findings, and conscious of the fact that decidua constitutes a major site of prostaglandin synthesis, we investigated the possibility that oxytocin may serve as a trigger to stimulate decidual prostaglandin synthesis and that this trigger could be mediated through oxytocin receptors (Fuchs *et al.* 1981).

Pieces of myometrium, decidua parietalis and amnion of 14 healthy pregnant women who had undergone a caesarean section at term (though with no prolonged labour, nor dystocia) were incubated under standardized conditions in Krebs-Ringer bicarbonate solution in an atmosphere of 95 per cent O_2 and 5 per cent CO_2 at 37 °C

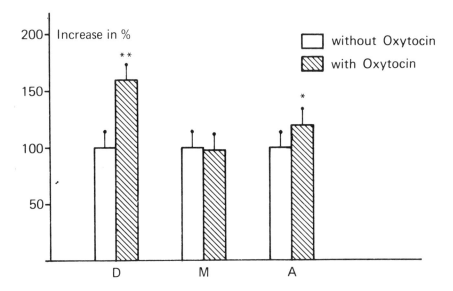

Figure 4. Influence of oxytocin on the production of prostaglandins PGE and PGF in vitro.

for 90 min with or without the addition of 10 ml IU oxytocin per ml of solution. The concentration of various prostanoids was determined in the supernatant and was expressed per mg dry weight. Fig. 4 shows the difference in prostaglandin output between tissues incubated with and without the addition of oxytocin. Decidual prostaglandin E and F production was clearly increased when oxytocin was present in the incubation medium, whereas myometrial prostaglandin production did not change. Amnion produced significantly more PGE in the presence of oxytocin, so that the increase in combined PGE + PGF production also reached statistical significance.

From these *in vitro* results we formulated the hypothesis that oxytocin may exert a dual action, producing myometrial contractions through receptors in the myometrium and increasing prostaglandin production in the decidua through receptors in the decidua parietalis.

Plasma studies

In order to test this hypothesis *in vivo* we determined the concentration of PGFM in the maternal peripheral plasma before and during induction of labour by intravenous oxytocin, which was infused at an increasing rate until regular contractions were present in all women. Fig. 5 shows that PGFM levels rose significantly in women where oxytocin led not only to regular contractions but also to progressive cervical

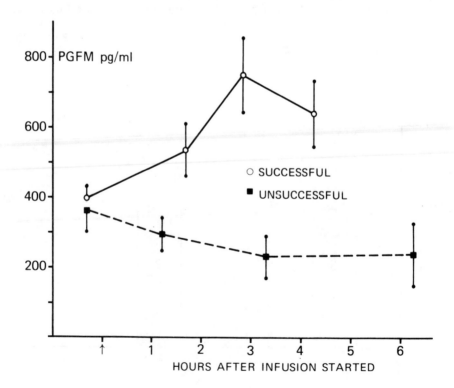

Figure 5. Plasma levels of PGFM during the induction of labour with oxytocin.

dilatation and finally vaginal delivery. In the induction failure group where, despite regular contractions, vaginal delivery could not be achieved and caesarean section had to be performed, the mean PGFM levels did not change (Husslein *et al.* 1981, Fuchs *et al.* 1983). In most of these women myometrial and decidual samples were obtained during caesarean section for oxytocin receptor determination and, as predicted from our hypothesis, decidual receptor concentrations were lower than in a comparable group of term patients. We concluded that oxytocin was not apparently able to stimulate prostaglandin production in this group of failed induction patients because of a lack of adequate numbers of oxytocin binding sites in the decidua. These results provide strong *in vivo* evidence in favour of our hypothesis.

In addition to arguments about the validity of radioimmunoassays, a major criticism relating to most studies in which oxytocin was determined before or during labour has been the lack of serial determinations possibly required to detect oxytocin spurts. In order to validate our RIA for oxytocin we measured plasma levels serially in 15 subjects during induction of labour with oxytocin (Fuchs *et al.* 1983). Fig. 6 shows that plasma oxytocin levels are directly correlated with the quantity of oxytocin infused. Moreover, the results obtained at infusion rates of 1–9 mIU/min are comparable to those measured during the first stage of spontaneous labour. Serial

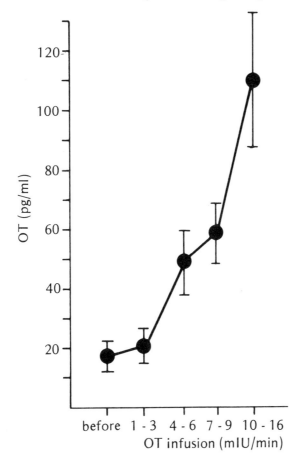

Figure 6. Plasma oxytocin levels before and during intravenous infusion of oxytocin for the induction of labour.

Table 2

Plasma oxytocin levels during term labour, mean $\pm SE$, serial
samples, pg/ml

Sample	Interval (h)	Oxytocin level	n
Control	Before labour	$23 \pm 5 \cdot 3$	26
1	Early labour	$40 \cdot 2 \pm 6 \cdot 9^a$	18
2	$2 \cdot 1 \pm 0 \cdot 3$	$42 \cdot 6 \pm 8 \cdot 0^a$	17
3	$2 \cdot 7 \pm 1 \cdot 1$	$47 \cdot 8 \pm 9 \cdot 4^a$	16
4	$2 \cdot 2 \pm 0 \cdot 3$	$46 \cdot 8 \pm 9 \cdot 0^a$	13

[a] Significantly different from control values, $p < 0 \cdot 05$

comparison of plasma oxytocin values in early labour with those in a control group of women not in labour show a clear and statistically significant difference already apparent at a very early stage (Table 2).

The following summary hypothesis was therefore formulated to explain the role of oxytocin in the mechanism of human labour (Fuchs *et al.* 1982, Husslein *et al.* 1982, Fuchs 1983a, 1983b, Husslein 1984). In the later part of human pregnancy a small increase in maternal oxytocin plasma levels can be observed which is difficult to detect in the peripheral plasma. The readiness of the foetus to be born is signalled by an increased secretion of oxytocin (and perhaps by other changes). Dawood *et al.* (1978) showed a significant increase in oxytocin levels in umbilical vessels, with higher levels of the umbilical artery, whenever labour started spontaneously. This foetal oxytocin crosses the placenta adding the equivalent of approximately 3 mIU of oxytocin/min to the maternal blood. This is sufficient to exceed the threshold of the myometrium which has dramatically fallen during the last days of pregnancy, associated with a significant rise in oxytocin receptor concentration leading to a marked increase in sensitivity. At the same time oxytocin binds to receptors in the decidua thereby stimulating prostaglandin synthesis, which in turn leads to further stimulation of myometrial contractions, softening of the cervix and formation of gap junctions finally leading to cervical dilatation and delivery.

Since the mechanism of labour is so vital for the survival of mankind it is unlikely to be based on only one chain of events. Several mechanisms are likely to be interlinked in order to guarantee its smooth and effective function. One reason why various research groups are in disagreement about the subject is that each of them may be looking at human labour only from a somewhat restricted perspective.

References

Caldeyro-Barcia, R. and Sereno, J. A. (1961). The response of the human uterus to oxytocin throughout pregnancy. In *Oxytocin*. Proceedings of an International Symposium. (Eds R. Caldeyro-Barcia and H. Heller) Montevideo, 1959. Pergamon Press, Oxford, p. 177.

Chard, T., Boyd, N. R. H., Forsling, M. L., McNeilly, A. S. and Landon, J. (1970). The development of a radioimmunoassay for oxytocin. The extraction of oxytocin from plasma and its measurement during parturition in human and goat blood. *Journal of Endocrinology* **43**, LXI.

Dawood, M. Y., Raghavan, K. S., Pociask, C. and Fuchs, F. (1978). Oxytocin in human pregnancy and parturition. *Obstetrics and Gynecology* **51**, 138.

Dawood, M. Y., Wang, C. F., Gupta, R. and Fuchs, F. (1978). Fetal contribution to oxytocin in human labor. *Obstetrics and Gynecology* **521**, 205.

Dawood, M. Y. (1983). Neurohypophyseal hormones. In *Endocrinology of pregnancy* 3rd Edition (Eds F. Fuchs and A. Klopper). Harper and Row, p. 204.

Fuchs, A. R. (1983a). The role of oxytocin in parturition. In *Current topics in experimental endocrinology*, vol. 4 (Eds L. Martini and V. James). p. 231.

Fuchs, A. R., Fuchs, F., Husslein, P., Fernström, M. and Soloff, M. S. (1984). Oxytocin receptors in pregnant human uterus and the regulation of oxytocin action during pregnancy and parturition. *American Journal of Obstetrics and Gynecology* **150**, 734.

Fuchs, A. R., Fuchs, F., Husslein, P., Soloff, M. S. and Fernström, M. J. (1982). Oxytocin receptors and human parturition: a dual role of oxytocin in the initiation of labor. *Science* **215**, 1396.

Fuchs, A. R., Goeschen, K., Husslein, P., Rasmussen, A. B. and Fuchs, F. (1983). Oxytocin and the initiation of human parturition III. Plasma concentrations of oxytocin and 13,14-dihydro-15-keto-prostaglandin F2-alpha in spontaneous and oxytocin-induced labor at term. *American Journal of Obstetrics and Gynecology* **147**, 479.

Fuchs, A. R., Husslein, P. and Fuchs, F. (1981). Oxytocin and the initiation of human parturition II. Stimulation of prostaglandin production in human decidua by oxytocin. *American Journal of Obstetrics and Gynecology* **141**, 694.

Fuchs, A. R., Husslein, P., Sumulong, L., Micha, J. P., Dawood, M. Y. and Fuchs, F. (1982). Plasma levels of oxytocin and 13,14-dihydro-15-keto-prostaglandin-F2-alpha in preterm labor and the effect of ethanol and ritodrine. *American Journal of Obstetrics and Gynecology* **144**, 753.

Fuchs, A. R., Periyasami, S., Alexandrova, M. and Soloff, M. S. (1983). Correlation between oxytocin receptor concentration and responsiveness to oxytocin in pregnant rat myometrium: effects of ovarian steroids. *Endocrinology* **113**, 742.

Fuchs, F. (1983b). Endocrinology of parturition. In *Endocrinology of parturition*, 3rd edition (Eds F. Fuchs and A. Klopper). Harper and Row, p. 247.

Gibbens, D., Boyd, N. R. H. and Chard, T. (1972). Spurt release of oxytocin during human labor. *Journal of Endocrinology* **53**, LIV.

Husslein, P. (1984). Die Bedeutung von Oxytocin und Prostaglandinen für den Geburtsmechanismus beim Menschen. *Weiner Klinische Wochenschrift* **96** (Suppl. 155).

Husslein, P., Fuchs, A. R. and Fuchs, F. (1981). Oxytocin and the initiation of human parturition. I. Prostaglandin release during induction of labor by oxytocin. *American Journal of Obstetrics and Gynecology* **141**, 688.

Husslein, P., Fuchs, A. R., Soloff, M. S. and Fuchs, F. (1982). Initiiert Fetales Oxytocin den Geburtsbeginn beim Menschen? Eine Hypothese. *Geburtshilfe und Frauenheilkunde* **42**, 579.

Kofler, E., Husslein, P., Langer, M., Fuchs, A. R. and Fuchs, F. (1983). Due Bedeutung der Oxytocinempfindlichkeit fur den spontanen wehenbeginn beim Menschen. *Geburtshilfe und Frauenheilkunde* **9**, 533.

Kumaresan, P., Han, G. S., Anadragam, P. B. and Vasicka, A. (1975). Oxytocin in maternal and fetal blood. *Obstetrics and Gynecology* **46**, 273.

Leake, R. D., Weitzmann, R. E., Glatz, T. H. and Fisher, D. A. (1981). Plasma oxytocin concentrations in men, nonpregnant women, and pregnant women before and during spontaneous labor. *Journal of Clinical Endocrinology and Metabolism* **53**, 730.

Sakamoto, J., Den, K., Yamoto, K., Arai, T., Kawai, S., Oyama, Y., Yoshida, T. and Takagi, S. (1979). Study of oxytocin receptor in human myometrium using highly specific (eH) labelled oxytocin. *Endocrinologica Japonica* **26**, 575.

Sellers, S. M., Hodgson, H. T., Mountford, L. A., Mitchell, M. D., Anderson, A. B. M. and Turnbull, A. C. (1981). Is oxytocin involved in parturition? *British Journal of Obstetrics and Gynaecology* **88**, 725.

Discussion

Dr Challis noted that in the group of patients with an unsuccessful oxytocin induction the oxytocin receptor population was depleted, though the amount of uterine contractility was similar to that of the successful group. He wondered if this was the explanation for their reduced level of prostaglandin generation.

Dr Husslein said that it was the *dedicual* receptor population that was very low in the non-successful group. Although the differences did not reach significance, it was striking to find normal concentrations of oxytocin receptors in the myometrium but much lower concentrations in the decidua. It therefore seemed that contractions could be induced at a myometrial level but the reason for reduced prostaglandin synthesis might well be the reduction in decidual oxytocin receptors.

Dr MacKenzie wondered whether there were any differences in receptor concentrations at various stages of labour in tissues taken from women at caesarean section.

Dr Husslein said that when they had looked for oxytocin receptors in very late labour, at full dilatation, they had found almost none. At first they had considered this to be a down-regulation process but later realized that it was a consequence of the time of the section. In late labour the uterus was retracted and the incision was made close to the cervix. Caesarean hysterectomy specimens had shown more receptors in the fundus and corpus than the isthmus, but the more closely one approached the cervix the less frequent the receptors became. Failure to find them in late labour therefore resulted from altered uterine anatomy.

Dr Calder remarked that the most dramatic increase in oxytocin sensitivity in the uterus resulted from amniotomy, which was associated with a massive release of prostaglandins.

Dr Husslein had conducted a study somewhat similar to those done in Oxford in which membranes were ruptured and oxytocin and prostaglandin levels measured. At one time amniotomy (ARM) had been regularly performed in his Department but only after an oxytocin sensitivity test, since the probability of labour after amniotomy was high in these instances, but low oxytocin sensitivity in that situation might produce problems. What they found, however, was little change in oxytocin levels following rupture of the membranes. Following ARM all patients showed a rise in the prostaglandin F metabolite and in those women who would go into labour the levels stayed high after 2 h. In the other group, after a transient rise levels fell again and such women would require oxytocin supplementation or caesarean section. They had therefore concluded that the results of amniotomy were mediated through some mechanism related to prostaglandin and not oxytocin. The fact that oxytocin sensitive patients responded better to amniotomy might result from some independent maturational event and the behaviour of oxytocin receptor and prostaglandin concentrations after rupturing the membranes might be independent events.

Dr Calder wondered whether endogenous prostaglandins might influence the development of oxytocin receptors.

Dr Husslein said that the only data on agents stimulating oxytocin receptors came from rats, where it had been clearly shown that they were under the influence of steroid hormone levels. An increase in oestrogen and a fall in progesterone stimulated an increase in oestrogen receptors with a rise in oxytocin receptors the following day. However, the problems of measuring oestrogen and progesterone receptors in the human myometrium had defeated their efforts and those of other research groups.

Biosynthesis and metabolism of prostaglandins within the human uterus in early and late pregnancy

M. J. N. C. KEIRSE

*Department of Obstetrics and Gynaecology,
University of Leiden Medical Centre, Netherlands*

There is now substantial evidence that prostaglandins are of critical importance in the initiation and maintenance of human labour (Keirse 1979b, Huszar and Naftolin 1984). The concentrations of prostaglandins and prostaglandin metabolites in plasma and amniotic fluid are unchanged throughout most of pregnancy, increased concentrations being found consistently only at the onset of and during labour. Detailed analysis of the pertinent literature is available elsewhere (Keirse 1979a). It is well established that the concentrations of PGE_2, $PGF_{2\alpha}$, its major metabolite (PGFM) and arachidonic acid in amniotic fluid are all increased at the onset of labour and that thereafter concentrations are correlated significantly with cervical dilatation and thence with progression of labour (Keirse 1979a). Mechanical procedures such as sweeping of the membranes (Mitchell *et al.* 1977a), amniotomy (Mitchell *et al.* 1977b) or intrauterine insertion of foreign bodies (Keirse *et al.* 1983, Manabe *et al.* 1982) which provoke labour are all known to evoke prostaglandin production mostly, as demonstrated recently, before the onset of uterine contractions (Keirse *et al.* 1983). Moreover, it has been demonstrated that, in women destined to require oxytocin acceleration of labour, amniotic fluid prostaglandin concentrations are significantly lower than in women who will labour successfully without intervention (Keirse *et al.* 1977b).

Thus, it seems likely that an enhanced rate of (intra)uterine prostaglandin production is a prerequisite for the normal physiological progression of labour (Keirse 1983). In addition, it is well recognized that prostaglandins are local mediators which are produced, when needed, in close proximity to their site of action and which are usually metabolized before they have an opportunity to affect other organ systems (Keirse 1979b). Consequently, there has been much research on the capacity of the pregnant uterus, and its contents, to synthesize and metabolize prostaglandins, in order to obtain a better understanding of the biochemical and physiological events leading to initiation and maintenance of labour.

The biosynthetic pathways of prostaglandin formation may be simplified into

*The role of prostaglandins in labour, edited by Clive Wood, 1985: Royal Society of Medicine Services
International Congress and Symposium Series No. 92, published by Royal Society of Medicine Services
Limited.*

two parts. Firstly, nonesterified arachidonic acid is released from lipid stores, glycerophospholipids in particular, and secondly, the arachidonic acid so generated is converted into prostaglandins. Catabolism of prostaglandins to inactive metabolites then forms a third mechanism whereby prostaglandin concentrations can be controlled. Each of these mechanisms will be considered briefly in the next section. The following two sections will then be devoted to the beginning and the end of gestation to specifically address two questions. First, how does prostaglandin biosynthesis and metabolism evolve in early pregnancy? Second, how is prostaglandin production in late pregnancy controlled at the myometrial level, which is—after all—the main target for the prostaglandins that are produced during parturition? In addressing these issues, I shall draw mainly on the results of our ongoing parturitional research instead of providing an exhaustive review of the appropriate literature.

General aspects of uterine prostaglandin biosynthesis and metabolism

Despite intense research there is still little agreement on how the increase in (intra)uterine prostaglandin production is brought about. Neither is it clear which of the (intra)uterine tissues provides the most vital contribution to uterine prostaglandin production in pregnancy and parturition.

Esterified arachidonic acid is an important constituent of all (intra)uterine tissues, accounting for between 9 and 26 per cent of the total fatty acid content of foetal membranes, placenta, umbilical cord, decidua and myometrium (Keirse 1975). All of these tissues contain various lipases, which can effect release of free arachidonic acid that is essential for prostaglandin biosynthesis; arachidonic acid was thus shown to account for 7 to 20 per cent of all free fatty acids in the various (intra)uterine tissues (Keirse 1978).

There is wide consensus that phospholipases in particular play an important role in making arachidonic acid available for prostaglandin biosynthesis, since in the (intra)uterine tissues much of the arachidonic acid is also contained in phospholipids (Keirse 1975). Evidence for a selective release of arachidonic acid from certain phospholipids in pregnancy and labour has been reviewed by Bleasdale *et al.* (1983). Nevertheless, it should be remembered that the control of free arachidonic acid in mammalian cells is a complex issue (Irvine 1982), that there are many mechanisms by which arachidonic acid can be released, and that not all arachidonic acid is necessarily directed toward prostaglandin biosynthesis but may also be turned toward lipoxygenase pathways (Taylor and Morris 1983), energy requirements (Van Dorp 1971) and, more important still, incorporation in the structural fat of cell membranes (Crawford 1983). This applies in particular to the pregnant uterus, wherein foetal needs for this essential fatty acid, structural requirements related to rapid (intra)uterine growth, and active transport to the foetus (Robertson and Sprecher 1968) all need to be considered (Keirse 1978).

Conversion of free arachidonic acid to prostaglandins depends in the first instance on the activity of prostaglandin endoperoxide synthase (PGH synthase), formerly known as cyclo-oxygenase. This enzyme, whose activity can be blocked by administration of prostaglandin synthesis inhibitors such as indomethacin and aspirin, is known to be present in all uterine tissues in late pregnancy (Christensen and Gréen 1983, Keirse 1979a, Willman and Collins 1976), but its relative distribution among these tissues has not been clearly established. It converts arachidonic acid to the prostaglandin endoperoxides, PGG_2 and subsequently PGH_2, which can then be converted enzymatically or non-enzymatically to the primary prostaglandins E_2, D_2 and $F_{2\alpha}$. The enzyme is known to be a glycoprotein (Van Der Ouderaa *et al.* 1977) whose activity *in vivo* is probably to a large extent dictated by cellular concentrations of hydroperoxides (Warso and Lands 1983).

While synthesis of PGH_2, albeit to different extents, is known to occur in all (intra)uterine tissues, evidence is presently accumulated that the further conversion to the various primary end-products (prostaglandins, prostacyclin and thromboxane) shows at least some specificity (Dembélé-Duchesne *et al.* 1981, Christensen and Gréen 1983, Keirse *et al.* 1985a). This implies that the further conversion of prostaglandin endoperoxides does indeed vary from tissue to tissue within the uterus (Keirse and Klok, unpublished observations), but this may, as it does in non-reproductive tissues (Sun *et al.* 1977), to some extent depend on the amount of prostaglandin endoperoxides that becomes available. As all of the classical primary prostaglandins can, at least *in vitro*, be formed from prostaglandin endoperoxides without the need of special enzymes, this is an important point to be made. For instance, no enzyme has yet been shown to catalyze the conversion of PGH_2 to $PGF_{2\alpha}$. Shortage or abundancy of prostaglandin endoperoxides can also affect the balance between TXA_2 and PGI_2, which do require separate enzymes — both of which seem to belong to the cytochrome P450 group (Ullrich and Graf, 1984) — in order to be produced.

There have been various reports on a chronic inhibition of prostaglandin production during pregnancy and its withdrawal at or during parturition. These were partially reviewed by Mitchell (1984); but, in general, corroborating evidence for their effect *in vivo* is still missing. Similarly, it has been postulated that factors contained in the cytosol of various intrauterine tissues (Saeed and Mitchell 1982) and elements present in amniotic fluid (Saeed *et al.* 1982) and in foetal urine (Strickland *et al.* 1983) can stimulate prostaglandin production in some, if not all, tissues. While these effects *in vitro* are not contested, it is at least dubious whether and to what extent they apply *in vivo*.

A similar note can be made regarding the catabolism of prostaglandins in (intra)uterine tissues. For instance, we (Keirse *et al.* 1976a & b) and others (Jarabak 1980) have shown that the capacity of the human placenta for inactivation of prostaglandins suffices to catabolize more prostaglandin per minute than would be administered per hour for the induction of labour. This certainly seems to indicate that this capacity is not likely to be used to its full extent *in vivo*. Nevertheless, it should presently be emphasized that all (intra)uterine tissues, albeit to different degrees, are capable of inactivating prostaglandins to metabolites that are devoid of uterotonic potencies (Keirse and Turnbull 1975, Keirse *et al.* 1975).

Thus, the entire system of enzymatic and non-enzymatic reactions that is required to both produce and inactivate prostaglandins is present throughout the pregnant uterus at term. While it is likely that this applies throughout most of pregnancy, it is not known how that capacity develops in early pregnancy.

Development of prostaglandin biosynthesis and metabolism in early gestation

Throughout most of pregnancy the human intrauterine environment is inaccessible to experimental designs of any other than a therapeutic nature. However, pregnancy terminations for social reasons provided us with an opportunity to study the evolution of prostaglandin biosynthesis and metabolism in the most characteristic tissue of pregnancy: the placenta. The methods used in these investigations are described in detail elsewhere and involved quantitation of PGH synthase and PGI_2 synthase with immunoradiometric assays using monoclonal antibodies against these enzymes (Moonen *et al.* 1984); preparation of the prostaglandin endoperoxide, PGH_2, from sheep vesicular glands (Van Der Ouderaa *et al.* 1977) and its use for investigating the bioconversion to prostaglandins, prostacyclin and thromboxane in microsomes, cytosol and homogenates of uterine tissues (Keirse *et al.* 1985a); development and use of a high pressure liquid chromatography system which allows resolution of thromboxane comparable to that of prostaglandins (Moonen *et al.* 1983) for on-line detection of the various end products formed from PGH_2; and quantitation of 15-hydroxy prostaglandin dehydrogenase (PGDH) activity in placental homogenates (Keirse *et al.* 1976b).

These investigations clearly showed that the capacity for both prostaglandin biosynthesis and prostaglandin catabolism increases significantly with placental development in early pregnancy from 7 up to at least 17 weeks of gestation. Concentrations of PGH synthase in placental microsomes increased on average about threefold between 7 weeks and the beginning of the second trimester of pregnancy (Keirse *et al.* 1985c). Surprisingly, however, there was no increase in PGI_2 synthase concentrations at that time. Unlike some other tissues, such as both pregnant and non-pregnant myometrium (Moonen *et al.* 1984), there was no evidence for an excess of PGI_2 synthase in comparison with PGH synthase concentrations (Keirse *et al.* 1985c).

Concentrations of PGDH also increased markedly, showing a tenfold increase in activity over the same range of gestation (Keirse *et al.* 1985b). It is noteworthy that the increase in PGDH activity was proportionally much greater than the increase in PGH synthase concentrations, although the latter cannot be assumed to equate with enzyme activities. In fact, when expressed per mg protein, PGDH activities already reached levels equal to those at term before the end of the first trimester (Fig. 1). This forms a marked contrast with our previous data (Keirse *et al.* 1976a & b) and

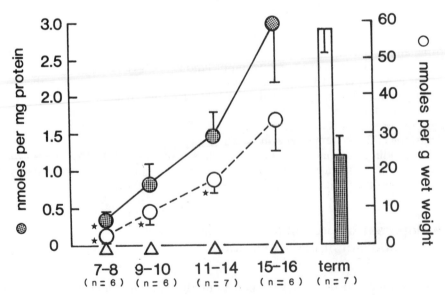

Figure 1. PGDH activities (mean ± SE nanomoles $PGF_{2\alpha}$ metabolized per min) per mg protein and per g wet weight in early as compared to term placentae. Asterisks indicate a statistical difference (Mann-Whitney rank sum test) with term values at $p < 0.01$. From Keirse et al. (1985b) with permission of Prostaglandins.

those of others (Jarabak 1980) which had thus far, and contrary to data in experimental animals (Keirse *et al.* 1977a), failed to detect meaningful correlations between clinical parameters and placental PGDH activity in late pregnancy. Although normal placentae are unlikely to become available for study in mid-pregnancy it would be of interest to know whether the trend seen up to 17 weeks is continued thereafter. Indeed, if it is, this would imply that there is then, later on, and well before the onset of labour is due to occur, a considerable fall in placental PGDH activity.

There has been considerable argument as to whether or not the main anti-aggregatory activity of the placenta is due to PGI_2 (Myatt and Elder 1977, Hutton *et al.* 1980), and as to whether the placenta does or does not produce PGI_2 (Jogee *et al.* 1983, Jeremy *et al.* 1985). While the former question has now been clearly answered in the negative (Hutton *et al.* 1980, Dembélé-Duchesnes *et al.* 1982), the latter is by no means resolved (Jeremy *et al.* 1985, Keirse *et al.* 1985c). This is of

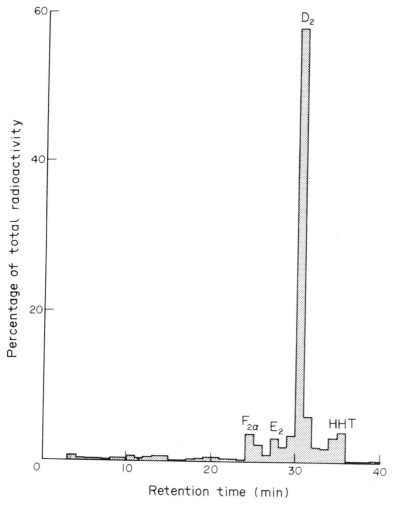

Figure 2. Conversion of ^{14}C-labeled prostaglandin endoperoxide, PGH_2, in placental cytosol at 15 weeks of gestation. Note the overwhelming predominance of PGD-isomerase which utilizes all available PGH_2 (HHT = 12-hydroxy-heptadecatrienoic acid). Percentage of total radioactivity (ordinate) plotted against retention time (min, abscissa).

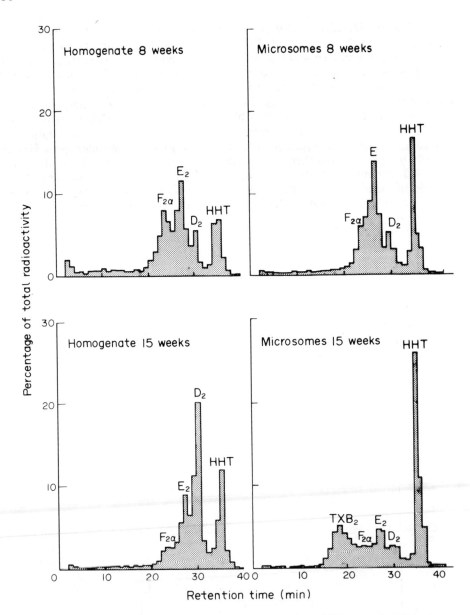

Figure 3. Comparison between the conversions of ^{14}C*-labeled* PGH_2 *in total homogenates and microsomal fractions of placentae obtained at 8 and 15 weeks of gestation. Note the marked conversion to thromboxane in microsomes and to* PGD_2 *in homogenates at 15 weeks as compared to a predominantly non-enzymatic decomposition of* PGH_2 *at 8 weeks of gestation (HHT = 12-hydroxy-heptadecatrienoic acid). Percentage of total radioactivity (ordinate) plotted against retention time (min, abscissa).*

relevance not only to the establishment of prostaglandin production in early pregnancy but also to the critical issue of whether prostacyclin is involved in the development of placentation as some have suggested (Lewis 1983) and consequently in the pathophysiology of conditions such as pregnancy-induced hypertension (Mäkilä *et al.* 1984), foetal growth retardation (Jogee *et al.* 1983) and other states of chronic placental insufficiency (Stuart *et al.* 1981), which have all been reputed to be associated with defective PGI_2 production.

Whereas we found that both early and late placentae contain PGI_2 synthase (Keirse *et al.* 1985c), we have thus far been unable to demonstrate bioconversion of PGH_2 into PGI_2 in either homogenates, microsomes or cytosol of placentae obtained at both early and late gestations (Keirse *et al.* 1985a). This is in accordance with data of Dembélé-Duchesnes *et al.* (1981 and 1982) and of Jeremy *et al.* (1985) who found placental PGI_2 production to be minimal if at all present, but not with the data of Jogee *et al.* (1983), who reported a significant output of the main prostacyclin metabolite, 6-keto $PGF_{1\alpha}$, from placental cells in culture.

In the course of these investigations we consistently recorded the capacity of placental homogenates to produce enzymatically another anti-aggregatory prostaglandin: PGD_2. Further investigation revealed the presence of a soluble PGD-isomerase in the cytosol of all placentae investigated except those obtained at or below 8 weeks of gestation. The activity of that enzyme became particularly predominant from about 15 weeks of gestation and remained so at term (Fig. 2). A similar evolution was found for another enzyme, thromboxane synthase, in the microsomal fraction of the placenta. Up to 8 weeks of gestation, no bioconversion of PGH_2 to thromboxane was observed in any of the placentae investigated (Fig. 3). Yet, from 10 weeks of gestation onwards it was consistently found in all placentae (Keirse *et al.* 1985a).

On the whole, our investigations have now provided conclusive evidence for marked developmental changes in placental prostaglandin biosynthesis and metabolism in early pregnancy. Two points about these changes in the placenta deserve particular attention. First, the changes involve several enzymes such as prostaglandin endoperoxide synthase (cyclo-oxygenase or PGH synthase), 15-hydroxy-prostaglandin dehydrogenase (PGDH), thromboxane synthase and PGD-isomerase, and, second, they do not all concur in time.

Control of prostaglandin biosynthesis at the myometrial level

Although it is generally accepted that the myometrium is the main target for the action of prostaglandins released during parturition, there has been remarkably little information on prostaglandin biosynthesis at the myometrial level. Such studies that have been conducted have, moreover, indicated that not a classical prostaglandin, but that prostacyclin (PGI_2) is the main arachidonic acid metabolite in pregnant myometrium (Christensen and Gréen 1983).

Attempts to ascribe a role to PGI_2 in the control of uterine contractility (Mitchell *et al.* 1978, Bamford *et al.* 1980) have been hampered by conflicting data on the effects of PGI_2 on myometrial contractility *in vitro* (Omini *et al.* 1979, Karim and Adaikan 1979, Wilhelmsson *et al.* 1981, Wikland *et al.* 1983) and the lack of reliable data *in vivo*. PGI_2 has been reported to be a tocolytic agent in some species such as the sheep (Lye and Challis 1982), but there are notorious differences between these species and man with regard to both the effects and metabolism of prostaglandins (Keirse *et al.* 1978). It has been suggested (Christensen and Gréen 1983) that the predominance of PGI_2 production in the myometrium relates to its high vascularity, but a similar predominance of PGI_2 production has been reported for non-pregnant myometrium (Abel and Kelly 1979).

Having demonstrated that both myometrial microsomes and homogenates indeed convert PGH_2 predominantly to PGI_2, we started a thorough investigation of prostaglandin endoperoxide synthase (PGH synthase) and PGI_2 synthase concentrations in pregnant myometrium in late pregnancy with a view to addressing several questions. First, how do PGH synthase and PGI_2 synthase concentrations compare with those in non-pregnant myometrium? Second, are there changes in enzyme concentrations with gestational age or with the onset of labour in late pregnancy? Third, what changes if any occur in pregnancy-induced hypertension, a state reputed to be associated with PGI_2 deficiency? Fourth, are these enzymes truly of myometrial origin or do they, as suggested by Christensen and Gréen (1983), reflect the extent of myometrial vascularization? Fifth, are these enzymes evenly distributed throughout the myometrium? The investigations were based on immunoradiometric assays of PGH synthase and PGI_2 synthase in myometrial microsomes (Moonen et al. 1984), on the bioconversion of ^{14}C-labeled PGH_2 in homogenates and subcellular fractions (Keirse and Klok, unpublished observations) and on immunohistochemical localization of the enzymes in cryotome sections (Moonen et al. 1985).

It was thus demonstrated that pregnant myometrium contained on average three times more PGH synthase than non-pregnant myometrium (Moonen et al. 1984). In myometrial microsomes, there was no significant increase in PGI_2 synthase in pregnancy as compared to the non-pregnant state, but significantly more PGI_2 synthase was recovered in non-microsomal fractions, thus providing evidence for a different subcellular distribution of PGI_2 synthase in pregnancy (Moonen et al. 1984). The reasons for this are unknown, but it was clearly demonstrated that this cannot be attributed entirely to the extent of myometrial vascularization, for the PGI_2 synthase antigen was located predominantly not in myometrial blood vessels but in the smooth muscle cells themselves (Keirse et al. 1984). In both pregnant and non-pregnant myometrium there was an excess of microsomal PGI_2 synthase over that of PGH synthase, but the relative proportions of these enzymes changed from

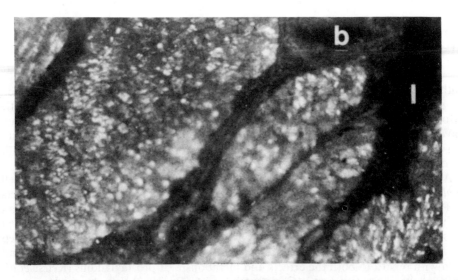

Figure 4. Immunohistochemical localization of the PGH synthase antigen in uterine smooth muscle in late pregnancy. Transverse section through smooth muscle fibres showing specific staining predominantly in the uterine smooth muscle but not in lymphatic (l) and blood (b) vessels. From Moonen et al. (1985) with permission of the European Journal of Obstetrics, Gynecology and Reproductive Biology.

20:1 in the non-pregnant state to 10:1 at the end of pregnancy. Nevertheless, there was no evidence for an increase in PGH synthase over the last few weeks of pregnancy nor with the onset of labour (Moonen *et al.* 1984). Similarly, there were no changes in PGI_2 synthase concentrations at that time of gestation or with labour. Neither could we find any decrease in the concentrations of either PGI_2 synthase or PGH synthase in the myometrium of patients with severe pregnancy-induced hypertension (Keirse *et al.* 1985d).

While immunohistochemical localization of the PGH synthase (Fig. 4) and PGI_2 synthase antigens had clearly shown that both of these enzyme were located predominantly in the smooth muscle itself (Moonen *et al.* 1985), we still found major differences in the enzyme concentration between different regions of a primigravid uterus removed at 34 weeks of gestation because of cervical carcinoma.

Analysis of samples taken at varying distances from the fundus and at various depths underneath the placental bed revealed several trends (Keirse *et al.* 1985e). First, PGH synthase concentrations in the outer half of the myometrium increased gradually, but markedly, from the uterine fundus toward the lower segment. Second, in myometrium underneath the placental bed, PGH synthase concentrations increased significantly from outer to inner layer and thus with increasing proximity to the placental bed. Third, PGI_2 synthase concentrations were significantly higher on the placental side of the uterus than on the contralateral side, but, contrary to PGH synthase concentrations, they showed no further increase with increasing proximity to the placental bed. Fourth, in samples obtained at various depths underneath the placental bed there was a significant, inverse relationship between the concentrations of PGH synthase and those of PGI_2 synthase. However, that negative correlation did not apply to other regions of the uterus and, in fact, this trend was the opposite of what we observed with cross-sectional data on lower segment myometrium from different patients. In the latter, there was instead a positive correlation between the concentrations of PGH synthase and those of PGI_2 synthase (Moonen *et al.* 1984).

Although the trends that have been described were highly significant ($p < 0.01$), it must be borne in mind that these data refer to one patient only at 34 weeks of gestation and well before the onset of labour. In addition, they relate to the antigenic properties of the PGH and PGI_2 synthase molecules and it cannot be assumed that all of the latter are of necessity present in an active or non-inhibited form. Nevertheless, we believe it to be unlikely that these large discrepancies between the localizations of PGI_2 synthase and PGH synthase are a mere anomaly without physiological significance. In accordance with current views, an explanation for these findings could be sought in terms of the control of placental irrigation or the modulation of uterine contractility.

Thus, the higher concentration of PGI_2 synthase on the placental as compared with the non-placental side of the uterus tie in with the classical view of PGI_2 as a prostaglandin of predominantly vascular origin (Moncada and Vane 1979), with higher vascularity underneath the placenta and with the capacities of PGI_2 as a vasodilator and promotor of organ perfusion (Lewis and Dollery 1983). However, the concentration gradient of PGI_2 synthase underneath the placental bed, its predominance in myometrial rather than in vascular structures (Keirse *et al.* 1984) and data which showed PGI_2 synthase to be a constituent enzyme of several types of smooth muscle (Smith *et al.* 1983), all indicate that the explanation is not likely to be as simple as that. Similarly, current hypotheses on the modulation of uterine contractility afford no straightforward explanation for these findings either. However, with regard to the effects on uterine contractility, there are other observations of marked differences between different regions of the pregnant uterus. For instance, Runnebaum and Zander (1971) showed progesterone concentrations to be several-fold higher in myometrium underneath the placenta than in sites remote from it. Fuchs *et al.* (1982) demonstrated a decreasing gradient of oxytocin receptors from corpus to lower uterine segment. Embrey and Morrison (1968) found large differences in the sensitivity to prostaglandins between myometrial strips from upper and lower segments and similar findings were reported for the *in vitro* sensitivity to prostacyclin (Wikland *et al.* 1983).

The main conclusion thus far seems to be that biosynthesis of prostaglandin endoperoxides and thence of prostaglandins and PGI_2 in the myometrium may be more dependent on intrauterine and anatomical relationships than has heretofore been realized.

Conclusions

Although the capacity of some, if not all, (intra)uterine tissues to both produce and metabolize prostaglandins has been known for some years, knowledge of the enzymatic processes within the uterus that produce these effects has lagged behind. The presented data have been selected as being exemplary for changes that occur at this level in early and late gestation. On the whole, they illustrate the complexity of interactions that govern (intra)uterine prostaglandin synthesis and they indicate that these processes undergo major changes during pregnancy. Full understanding of these changes and of the location, concentration and activity of the enzymes involved, may, some day, provide the clinical tools that are needed to ensure a better and adequate control of gestational length.

Acknowledgments

I am grateful to Drs J. J. Erwich, Ms G. Klok, Dr P. Moonen, Dr W. Noort, Ms H. Wittenberg and Mr F. de Zwart who made valuable contributions to the work described herein. Professor W. L. Smith, Department of Biochemistry, Michigan State University, USA, generously provided antibodies used in these studies, which were supported by the Netherlands Foundation for Medical Research (FUNGO, Grant 13-44-42) and the Praeventiefonds, The Hague (Grant 28-1118).

References

Abel, M. H. and Kelly, R. W. (1979). Differential production of prostaglandins within the human uterus. *Prostaglandins* **18**, 821.
Bamford, D. S., Jogee, M. and Williams, K. I. (1980). Prostacyclin formation by the pregnant human myometrium. *British Journal of Obstetrics and Gynaecology* **87**, 215.
Bleasdale, J. E., Okazaki, T. Sagawa, N., Di Renzo, G. C., Okita, J. R., MacDonald, P. C. and Johnston, J. M. (1983). The mobilization of arachidonic acid for prostaglandin production during parturition. In: *Initiation of parturition: prevention of prematurity*. Report of the Fourth Ross Conference on Obstetric Research. (Eds P. C. MacDonald and J. Porter) Ross Laboratories, Columbus, Ohio. p. 129.

Christensen, N. J. and Gréen, K. (1983). Bioconversion of arachidonic acid in human pregnant reproductive tissues. *Biochemical Medicine* **30**, 162.

Crawford, M. A. (1983). Background to essential fatty acids and their prostanoid derivatives. *British Medical Bulletin* **39**, 210.

Dembélé-Duchesne, M. J., Thaler-Dao, H., Chavis, C. and Crastes de Paulet, A. (1981). Some new prospects in the mechanism of control of arachidonate metabolism in human placenta and amnion. *Prostaglandins* **22**, 979.

Dembélé-Duchesne, M. J., Thaler-Dao, H., Chavis, C. and Crastes de Paulet, A. (1982). The human placental anti-aggregating factor is neither prostacyclin nor a prostacyclin metabolite. *Prostaglandins* **24**, 701.

Embrey, M. P. and Morrison, D. L. (1968). The effect of prostaglandins on human pregnant myometrium in vitro. *Journal of Obstetrics and Gynaecology of the British Commonwealth* **75**, 829.

Fuchs, A.-R., Fuchs, F., Husslein, P., Soloff, M. S. and Fernström, M. (1982). Oxytocin receptors and human parturition. A dual role for oxytocin in the initiation of labor. *Science* **215**, 1396.

Huszar, G. and Naftolin, F. (1984). The myometrium and uterine cervix in normal and preterm labor. *New England Journal of Medicine* **311**, 571.

Hutton, R. A., Dandona, P., Chow, F. P. and Craft, I. L. (1980). Inhibition of platelet aggregation by placental extracts. *Thrombosis Research* **17**, 465.

Irvine, R. F. (1982). How is the level of free arachidonic acid controlled in mammalian cells? *Biochemical Journal* **204**, 3.

Jarabak, J. (1980). Early steps in prostaglandin metabolism in the human placenta. *American Journal of Obstetrics and Gynecology* **138**, 534.

Jeremy, J. Y., Barradas, M. A., Craft, I. L., Mikhailidis, D. P. and Dandona, P. (1985). Does human placenta produce prostacyclin? *Placenta* **6**, 45.

Jogee, M., Myatt, L. and Elder, M. G. (1983). Decreased prostacyclin production by placental cells in culture from pregnancies complicated by fetal growth retardation. *British Journal of Obstetrics and Gynaecology* **90**, 247.

Karim, S. M. M. and Adaikan, P. G. (1979). Some pharmacological studies with prostacyclin in baboon and man. In: *Prostacyclin*. (Eds J. R. Vane and S. Bergström). Raven Press, New York, p. 419.

Keirse, M. J. N. C. (1975). *Studies in prostaglandins in relation to human parturition*. D.Phil. Thesis, University of Oxford.

Keirse, M. J. N. C. (1978). Biosynthesis and metabolism of prostaglandins in the pregnant human uterus. *Advances in Prostaglandin and Thromboxane Research* **4**, 87.

Keirse, M. J. N. C. (1979a). Endogenous prostaglandins in human parturition. In: *Human parturition, new concepts and developments* (Eds M. J. N. C. Keirse, A. B. M. Anderson and J. Bennebroek Gravenhorst). Leiden University Press, The Hague, p. 101.

Keirse, M. J. N. C. (1979b). Prostaglandines et déclenchement spontané du travail. In: *Les prostaglandines et la réproduction humaine* (Ed. J. J. Amy). Flammarion, Paris. p. 107.

Keirse, M. J. N. C. (1983). Prostaglandins during human parturition. In: *Initiation of parturition: prevention of prematurity*. Report of the Fourth Ross Conference on Obstetric Research (Eds P. C. MacDonald and J. Porter). Ross Laboratories, Columbus, Ohio. p 137.

Keirse, M. J. N. C. and Turnbull, A. C. (1975). Metabolism of prostaglandins within the pregnant uterus. *British Journal of Obstetrics and Gynaecology* **82**, 887.

Keirse, M. J. N. C., Williamson, J. G. and Turnbull, A. C. (1975). Metabolism of prostaglandin $F_{2\alpha}$ within the human uterus in early pregnancy. *British Journal of Obstetrics and Gynaecology* **82**, 142.

Keirse, M. J. N. C., Hanssens, M. C. A. J. A., Hicks, B. R. and Turnbull, A. C. (1976a). Prostaglandin metabolism in placenta and chorion before and after the onset of labor. *European Journal of Obstetrics, Gynecology and Reproductive Biology* **6**, 1.

Keirse, M. J. N. C., Hicks, B. R. and Turnbull, A. C. (1976b). Prostaglandin dehydrogenase in the placenta before and after the onset of labour. *British Journal of Obstetrics and Gynaecology* **83**, 152.

Keirse, M. J. N. C., Mitchell, M. D. and Flint, A. P. F. (1977a). Changes in myometrial and placental 15-hydroxy-prostaglandin dehydrogenase with ovine parturition: production of prostaglandin metabolites *in vitro* and *in vivo*. *Journal of Reproduction and Fertility* **51**, 409.

Keirse, M. J. N. C., Mitchell, M. D. and Turnbull, A. C. (1977b). Changes in prostaglandin F and 13,14-dihydro-15-keto-prostaglandin F in amniotic fluid at the onset of and during labour. *British Journal of Obstetrics and Gynaecology* **84**, 743.

Keirse, M. J. N. C., Hicks, B. R., Kendall, J. Z. and Mitchell, M. D. (1978). Comparison of intrauterine prostaglandin metabolism during pregnancy in man, sheep and guinea pig. *European Journal of Obstetrics, Gynecology and Reproductive Biology* **8**, 195.

Keirse, M. J. N. C., Thiery, M., Parewijck, W. and Mitchell, M. D. (1983). Chronic stimulation of uterine prostaglandin synthesis during cervical ripening before the onset of labor. *Prostaglandins* **25**, 671.

Keirse, M. J. N. C., Moonen, P. and Klok, G. (1984). Prostacyclin synthase in pregnant human myometrium is not confined to the utero-placental vasculature. *IRCS Medical Science* **12**, 824.

Keirse, M. J. N. C., Erwich, J. J. H. M. and Klok, G. (1985a). Bioconversion of prostaglandin endoperoxide in the human placenta of early and late gestation (submitted).

Keirse, M. J. N. C., Erwich, J. J. H. M. and Klok, G. (1985b). Increase in placental 15-hydroxy-prostaglandin dehydrogenase in the first half of human pregnancy. *Prostaglandins* **30**, 131.

Keirse, M. J. N. C., Erwich, J. J. H. M. and Klok, G. (1985c). Not prostacyclin synthase but prostaglandin endoperoxide synthase increases with human placental development (submitted).

Keirse, M. J. N. C., Moonen, P. and Klok, G. (1985d). Control of prostacyclin synthesis in pregnancy-induced hypertension. *Prostaglandins* **29**, 643.

Keirse, M. J. N. C., Moonen, P. and Klok, G. (1985e). The influence of uterine anatomy on the concentrations of prostaglandin endoperoxide and prostacyclin synthases during human pregnancy *European Journal of Obstetrics, Gynecology and Reproductive Biology* **19**, 327.

Lewis, P. J. (1983). Does prostacyclin deficiency play a role in preeclampsia? In: *Prostacyclin in pregnancy* (Eds P. J. Lewis, S. Moncada and J. O'Grady). Raven Press, New York, p. 215.

Lewis, P. J. and Dollery, C. T. (1983). Clinical pharmacology and potential of prostacyclin. *British Medical Bulletin* **39**, 281.

Lye, S. J. and Challis, J. R. G. (1982). Inhibition by PGI-2 of myometrial activity *in vivo* in non-pregnant ovariectomized sheep. *Journal of Reproduction and Fertility* **66**, 311.

Mäkilä, U.-M, Viinikka, L. and Ylikorkala, O. (1984). Evidence that prostacyclin deficiency is a specific feature in preeclampsia. *American Journal of Obstetrics and Gynecology* **148**, 772.

Manabe, Y., Manabe, A. and Takahashi, A. (1982). F prostaglandin levels in amniotic fluid during balloon-induced cervical softening and labor at term. *Prostaglandins* **23**, 247.

Mitchell, M. D. (1984). The mechanism(s) of human parturition. *Journal of Developmental Physiology* **6**, 107.

Mitchell, M. D., Flint, A. P. F., Bibby, J., Brunt, J., Anderson, A. B. M. and Turnbull, A. C. (1977a). Rapid increases in plasma prostaglandin concentrations after vaginal examination and amniotomy. *British Medical Journal* **2**, 1183.

Mitchell, M. D., Keirse, M. J. N. C., Anderson, A. B. M. and Turnbull, A. C. (1977b). Evidence for local control of prostaglandins within the pregnant human uterus. *British Journal of Obstetrics and Gynaecology* **84**, 35.

Mitchell, M. D., Bibby, J. G., Hicks, B. R. and Turnbull, A. C. (1978). Possible role for prostacyclin in human parturition. *Prostaglandins* **16**, 931.

Moncada, S. and Vane, J. R. (1979). Pharmacology and endogenous roles of prostaglandin endoperoxides, thromboxane A_2 and prostacyclin. *Pharmacological Reviews* **30**, 293.

Moonen, P., Klok, G. and Keirse, M. J. N. C. (1983). An improved method for separation of thromboxane B_2 by reversed phase liquid chromatography. *Prostaglandins* **26**, 797.

Moonen, P., Klok, G. and Keirse, M. J. N. C. (1984). Increase in concentrations of prostaglandin endoperoxide synthase and prostacyclin synthase in human myometrium in late pregnancy. *Prostaglandins* **28**, 309.

Moonen, P., Klok, G. and Keirse, M. J. N. C. (1985). Immunohistochemical localisation of prostaglandin endoperoxide synthase and prostacyclin synthase in pregnant human myometrium. *European Journal of Obstetrics, Gynecology and Reproductive Biology* **19**, 151.

Myatt, L. and Elder, M. (1977). Inhibition of platelet aggregation by a placental substance with prostacyclin-like activity. *Nature (London)* **268**, 159.

Omini, C., Folco, G. C., Pasargiklian, R., Fano, M. and Berti, F. (1979). Prostacyclin (PGI_2) in pregnant human uterus. *Prostaglandins* **17** 113.

Robertson, A. F. and Sprecher, H. (1968). A review of human placental lipid metabolism and transport. *Acta Paediatrica Scandinavica* Supplement **183**, 1.

Runnebaum, B. and Zander, J. (1971). Progesterone and 20α-dihydroprogesterone in human myometrium during pregnancy. *Acta Endocrinologica* Supplement 150.

Saeed, S. A. and Mitchell, M. D. (1982). Stimulants of prostaglandin biosynthesis in human fetal membranes, uterine decidua vera and placenta. *Prostaglandins* **24**, 475.

Saeed, S. A., Strickland, D. M., Young, D. C., Dang, A. and Mitchell, M. D. (1982). Inhibition of prostaglandin synthesis by human amniotic fluid: acute reduction in inhibitory activity of amniotic fluid obtained during labor. *Journal of Clinical Endocrinology and Metabolism* **55**, 801.

Smith, W. L., DeWitt, D. L. and Allen, M. L. (1983). Bimodal distribution of the prostaglandin I_2 synthase antigen in smooth muscle cells. *Journal of Biological Chemistry* **258**, 5922.

Strickland, D. M., Saeed, S. A., Casey, M. L. and Mitchell, M. D. (1983). Stimulation of prostaglandin biosynthesis by urine of the human fetus may serve as a trigger for parturition. *Science* **220**, 521.

Stuart, M. J., Clark, D. A., Sunderji, S. G., Allen, J. B., Yambo, T., Elrad, H. and Slott, J. H. (1981). Decreased prostacyclin production: a characteristic of chronic placental insufficiency syndromes. *Lancet* **1** 1126.

Sun, F. F., Chapman, J. P. and McGuire, J. C. (1977). Metabolism of prostaglandin endoperoxide in animal tissues. *Prostaglandins* **14**, 1055.

Taylor, G. W. and Morris, H. R. (1983). Lipoxygenase pathways. *British Medical Bulletin* **39**, 219.

Ullrich, V. and Graf, H. (1984). Prostacyclin and thromboxane synthase as P-450 enzymes. *Trends in Pharmacological Science* **5**, 352.

Van Der Ouderaa, F. J., Buytenhek, M., Nugteren, D. H. and Van Dorp, D. A. (1977). Purification and characterisation of prostaglandin endoperoxide synthetase from sheep vesicular glands. *Biochimica Biophysica Acta* **487**, 315.

Van Dorp, D. A. (1971). Essentielle Fettsaüren und Prostaglandine. In : *Fettstoffwechselstörungen ihre Erkennung und Behandlung* (Ed G. Schettler). Thieme, Stuttgart. p. 152.

Warso, M. A. and Lands, W. E. M. (1983). Lipid peroxidation in relation to prostacyclin and thromboxane physiology and pathophysiology. *British Medical Bulletin* **39**, 277.

Wikland, H., Lindblom, B., Hammarström, S. and Wiqvist, N. (1983). The effect of prostaglandin I_2 on the contractility of the term pregnant human myometrium. *Prostaglandins* **26**, 905.

Wilhelmsson, L., Wikland, M. and Wiqvisst, N. (1981). PGH_2, TXA_2 and PGI_2 have potent and differentiated actions on human uterine contractility. *Prostaglandins* **21**, 277.

Willman, E. A. and Collins, W. P. (1976). Distribution of prostaglandin E_2 and prostaglandin $F_{2\alpha}$ within the foetoplacental unit throughout human pregnancy. *Journal of Endocrinology* **69**, 413.

Discussion

Dr MacKenzie commented on the fact that most tissues seemed to metabolize prostaglandins except amniotic fluid and foetal blood.

Dr Keirse said that maternal blood did not metabolize them rapidly either. Erythrocytes were among the few cells of the body which did not possess significant 15-hydroxy prostaglandin dehydrogenase activity.

Dr Challis wondered whether human foetal cells possessed a 9-keto-reductase.

Dr Keirse said that, as far as he was aware, human foetal cells did not, in contrast to those in the foetal sheep.

Dr Calder said that this raised the question of the relative importance of the E and F series of prostaglandins, a topic to be discussed more extensively later.

Recent studies on the role of prostaglandins in parturition in sheep

WILLIAM LEIGH LEDGER

William Osler House,
John Radcliffe Hospital, Headington, Oxford, UK

Delivery of the foetus can only be achieved if uterine contractions of sufficient amplitude, duration and frequency are combined with adequate cervical softening and dilation. It is likely that prostaglandins (PGs) are involved in the regulation of both uterus and cervix during labour. Using the sheep as a model we have conducted experiments to investigate the actions of PGs during labour and the means by which uterine and cervical PG synthesis may be controlled.

It is possible that the cervix is capable of producing increasing amounts of PGs in response to changes in circulating concentrations of steroid hormones. Increases in concentrations of PGs within cervical tissues may initiate changes in the biochemistry of the cervical connective tissue which lead to the alterations in the mechanical properties of the cervix seen at term. Ellwood (1980) has shown that cervical tissue can produce appreciable quantities of PGs and that production of PGE and 6-keto $PGF_{1\alpha}$ was increased during labour.

Studies on isolated cervix

The aim of our first series of experiments was to determine whether the cervix of the pregnant sheep would soften during labour despite having been surgically isolated from the uterus. Surgical transection of the cervix was carried out under general anaesthesia on 8 ewes during late pregnancy. After careful dissection and ligation of superficial blood vessels, each cervix was bisected using a transverse incision. The greater part of the tissue was in connection with the vagina, with a smaller part attached to the uterus. Labour was then induced in 4 out of the 8 ewes by intra-foetal injection of dexamethasone, as described by Flint *et al.* (1974), the other 4 ewes being injected with saline.

Continuous monitoring of intra-uterine pressure changes using an intra-amniotic catheter showed the development of a pattern of uterine activity identical to that seen in normal labour in the ewes treated with dexamethasone, while no increases in uterine

The role of prostaglandins in labour, edited by Clive Wood, 1985: Royal Society of Medicine Services International Congress and Symposium Series No. 92, published by Royal Society of Medicine Services Limited.

Table 1
Cervical extensibility in isolated cervix

Treatment	Animal	Cervical extensibility (min^{-1}) at sacrifice
Dexamethasone	1	7·9
	2	10·9
	3	12·8
	4	12·1
Saline	5	4·0
	6	2·3
	7	2·6
	8	3·2

activity were seen in the animals treated with saline. Ewes were sacrificed 48 h after injection of dexamethasone or saline and the extensibility of the cervical tissue isolated from the uterus was determined in each case, using an apparatus described previously (Ledger *et al.* 1983). Results of these tests (Table 1) showed that despite being mechanically isolated from the uterus, the cervices of those animals in which labour had been induced had softened considerably in comparison to the controls. Thus it would appear that the cervix of the pregnant sheep can still undergo structural changes similar to those which precede normal delivery after being separated from any mechanical or local vascular connections with the uterus. If the prostaglandins are involved in cervical softening then it is likely that they are produced within the cervix itself.

Progesterone withdrawal

Treatment of late pregnant sheep with an inhibitor of 3β-hydroxysteroid dehydrogenase leads to a precipitate fall in the circulating concentration of progesterone and to the initiation of labour (Taylor *et al.* 1982). We have studied the effects of such treatment on the concentrations of stable metabolites of PGE and PGF measured in plasma collected from catheters implanted into the utero-ovarian vein in late pregnant sheep. The aim of this experiment was to study the effect of concurrent treatment with an inhibitor of PG synthesis on labour induced by progesterone withdrawal.

Eight ewes were treated with an inhibitor of 3β-hydroxysteroid dehydrogenase (Epostane™, Sterling Winthrop) during late pregnancy (Fig. 1). Four animals received concurrent infusions of mefenamic acid (MFA), an inhibitor of cyclo-oxygenase. The effect of injection of Epostane was to produce a rapid but transient fall in the concentration of progesterone in the utero-ovarian vein. This fall in the concentration of progesterone was not accompanied by any rise in the concentration of oestradiol-17β (Fig. 2).

The effect of Epostane on progesterone concentrations was not affected by infusion of mefenamic acid. In the animals which were treated with Epostane alone, progesterone withdrawal was followed by significant increases in the concentrations of metabolites of PGE and PGF in plasma from the utero-ovarian vein. Treatment with mefenamic acid abolished much of these increases (Fig. 3). Progesterone withdrawal alone was also followed by an increase in the level of uterine activity similar to that seen during normal labour.

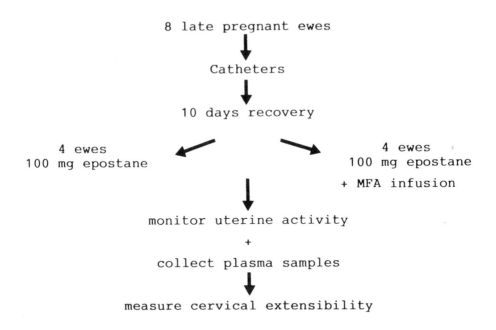

Figure 1. *Method used to study the effect of inhibition of PG synthesis on labour induced by progesterone withdrawal.*

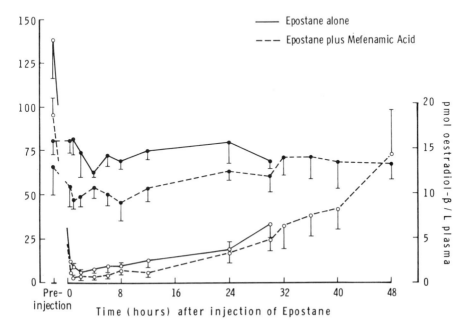

Figure 2. *Concentrations of progesterone (nmol/l plasma; open circles) and oestradiol-17β (pmol/l plasma; closed circles) in utero-ovarian venous plasma immediately before and at intervals after injection of Epostane alone (solid lines, n = 4) or in combination with infusion of mefenamic acid (broken lines, n = 4). Values are means ± SEM.*

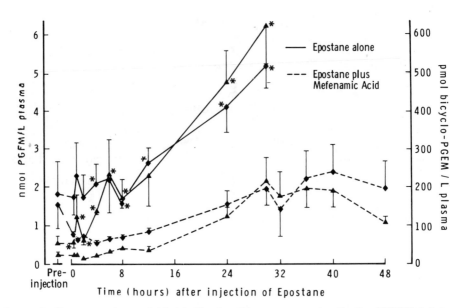

Figure 3. Concentrations of 13,14-dihydro-15-oxo-prostaglandin F_{2α} (PGFM) (▲) and 11-deoxy-13,14-dihydro-15-oxo-11β,16ε-cyclo PGE_2 (bicyclo-PGEM)(◆) in utero-ovarian venous plasma immediately before and at intervals after injection of Epostane alone (solid lines) or in combination with mefenamic acid (broken lines). *p < 0·02 compared with mefenamic acid values measured at the same time (Mann-Whitney test).

Once a pre-expulsive pattern of activity was clearly recognized the ewes were sacrificed and cervical extensibility determined as before. Ewes infused with mefenamic acid did not show any substantial increases in uterine activity and were sacrificed 48 h after injection of Epostane. Measurements of cervical extensibility (Table 2) showed that infusion of mefenamic acid had prevented the increases in extensibility seen after treatment with Epostane alone. The results suggest that uterine contractions and cervical softening can be induced by progesterone withdrawal and inhibited by inhibition of prostaglandin synthesis.

Table 2

Cervical extensibility following treatment with
Epostane (E) alone, or with mefenamic acid (E ± MF)

Treatment	Animal	Duration of experiment (h)	Cervical extensibility (min^{-1}) at sacrifice
E	1	32	16·0
E	2	33	14·5
E	3	35	13·6
E	4	32	10·8
E + MF	5	42	6·9
E + MF	6	48	6·6
E + MF	7	48	3·5
E + MF	8	48	4·0

References

Ellwood, D. A., Mitchell, M. D., Anderson, A. B. M. and Turnbull, A. C. (1980). Specific changes in the *in vitro* production of prostanoids by the ovine cervix at parturition. *Prostaglandins* **19**, 479.

Flint, A. P. F., Anderson, A. B. M., Patten, P. T. and Turnbull, A. C. (1974). Control of utero-ovarian venous prostaglandin F during labour in the sheep: acute effects of vaginal and cervical stimulation. *Journal of Endocrinology* **63**, 67.

Ledger, W. L., Ellwood, D. A. and Taylor, M. J. (1983). Cervical softening in late pregnant sheep by infusion of prostaglandin E₂ into a cervical artery. *Journal of Reproduction and Fertility* **69**, 511.

Taylor, M. J., Webb, R., Mitchell, M. D. and Robinson, J. S. (1982). Effect of progesterone withdrawal in sheep during late pregnancy. *Journal of Endocrinology* **92**, 85.

Discussion

Dr Calder said that the first experiment, interrupting the vascular connection between the uterus and cervix, suggested that some systemic endocrine phenomenon must be responsible for cervical changes. He wondered if that was progesterone.

Dr Ledger said that it was certainly possible that the cervix was responding in a similar way to the uterus to changes in the concentration of progesterone and oestradiol. However, he had not investigated the question further.

Dr Husslein said that the first set of experiments showed that cervical ripening could occur independently of uterine activity. West German studies had also shown that administering a prostaglandin-containing gel to the cervix and at the same time infusing the patient with beta-mimetics produced an increase in Bishop score with no demonstrable change in uterine contractility. He was therefore convinced that prostaglandins might act to reduce cervical resistance quite independent of any effect on uterine activity. However, in clinical practice he had found it impossible to produce such an exclusively cervical effect. There seemed to be no dose or route of application that would influence the cervix alone.

Dr Ledger said that was true in the human subject. In the sheep he had implanted catheters into a cervical artery and was therefore able to perfuse the cervix with prostaglandins. Giving PGE_2 infusions for 2 days they had been able to demonstrate an increase in cervical softening without any increase in uterine activity.

Dr MacKenzie said that giving Epostane and removing progesterone led to cervical softening, but he wondered whether there was any relationship between the state of the cervix and levels of circulating progesterone.

Dr Ledger said that again the situation differed between the human and the sheep. Cervical softening in the sheep occurred when progesterone was falling. Up to a few days before delivery the cervix remained hard.

Dr Calder said that progesterone inhibited collagenase activity in the myometrium and presumably in the cervix. He wondered how this related to cervical ripening.

Dr Ledger said that some specialists believed that changes in the cervix during parturition were caused by changes in collagen. Others attributed them to changes in the ground substance. He had held the latter view, though he currently felt that collagen changes might also be involved. He knew of no work on the effects of progesterone on the enzymes involved in ground substance changes, and until such investigations had been performed the work on collagenase was the only data they had relating to the topic.

Plasma concentrations of prostaglandins and oxytocin in labour

SUSAN SELLERS

Nuffield Department of Obstetrics and Gynaecology,
John Radcliffe Hospital, Headington, Oxford, UK

Circulating prostaglandin (PG) and oxytocin concentrations have been measured in spontaneous and induced labour. Plasma oxytocin concentrations showed a gradual rise with increasing gestation (Fig. 1) but there was no apparent increase just before the onset of labour. In our studies, maternal oxytocin concentrations did not change during the first and second stage of labour. However, examination

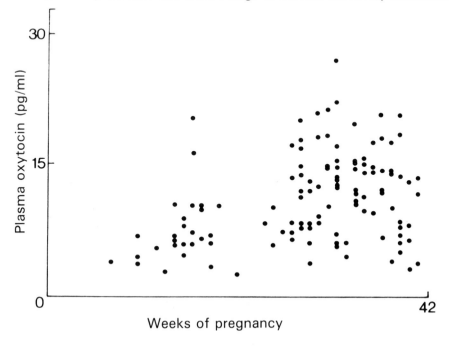

Figure 1. Plasma oxytocin levels during pregnancy

The role of prostaglandins in labour, edited by Clive Wood, 1985: Royal Society of Medicine Services International Congress and Symposium Series No. 92, published by Royal Society of Medicine Services Limited.

of oxytocin concentrations in umbilical cord blood did confirm the findings of others (Chard *et al.* 1971) that concentrations in the umbilical artery are significantly higher than in the vein with higher levels after spontaneous labour than at elective caesarean section.

The finding that amniotomy performed in late pregnancy causes a rapid increase in maternal plasma levels of 13,14-dihydro-15-keto prostaglandin $F_{2\alpha}$ (PGFM, the major circulating metabolite of $PGF_{2\alpha}$) is now well established. This work has been extended and PGFM concentrations have been measured 30 min after amniotomy for the induction of labour, and at hourly intervals thereafter up to 5 h. The 5 h period was chosen because it was felt that those patients who were not in established labour by that time required augmentation. Of the 16 women in the study, seven became established in labour during the sampling period, but the remaining nine patients did not, and received Syntocinon[TM] (oxytocin) to induce labour.

All women showed a significant rise in PGFM 5 min after amniotomy and the magnitude of the rise was the same in the two groups of patients. However, the subsequent changes followed a different pattern. In women who went into labour without oxytocin there was a significant increase in PGFM concentrations before 5 min and 30 min and a further significant increase between 30 min and the time at which the last sample was taken. However, in the group requiring oxytocin there was no significant difference in the PGFM concentrations at 30 min or at 5 h; in some patients the levels remained stable and in others they actually fell. It seems that following amniotomy some patients are suitably primed in terms of maturational events having occurred in the membranes, myometrium or decidua so that amniotomy leads to a secondary effect causing the onset of labour, whereas in other patients such events have not occurred.

The cause of the rise in prostaglandins that occurs after amniotomy is not understood but it is thought to be a local intrauterine mechanism. We have carried

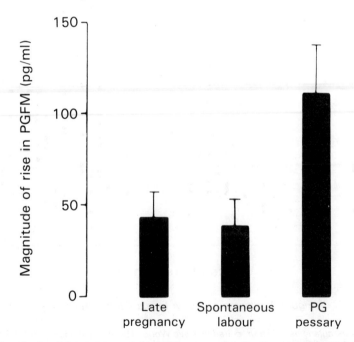

Figure 2. Magnitude of the rise in peripheral plasma concentrations of PGFM (mean ± SEM) at amniotomy.

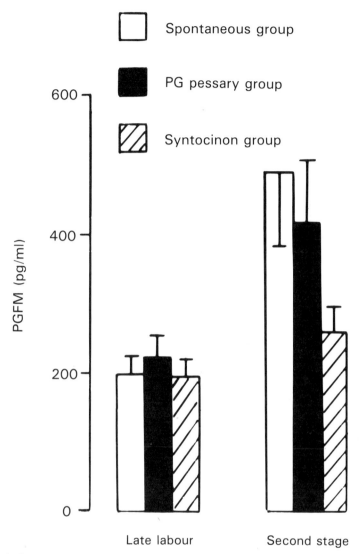

Figure 3. Comparison of plasma PGFM levels (mean ± SEM) in late and second stage labour.

out further studies to investigate the influence of spontaneous labour and of the administration of a PGE$_2$ vaginal pessary on the release of PGF following amniotomy in the hope that it might further our understanding of the factors controlling prostaglandin release. A significant increase in PGFM concentrations occurred in all groups ($p < 0.02$) or the spontaneous group ($p < 0.05$). However, no significant differences in the magnitude of the response were observed between the spontaneous group and the late pregnant controls (Fig. 2).

We have also measured maternal PGFM and oxytocin concentrations during labour induced either with a PGE$_2$ pessary or with Syntocinon and compared the results to the findings in spontaneous labour. The trends were similar in labour induced with prostaglandins or with Syntocinon. Unfortunately, in the spontaneous labour group we did not have sufficient patients in early labour (cervix less than 4 cm dilated) to make statistical analyses. The majority of women were in late labour on admission

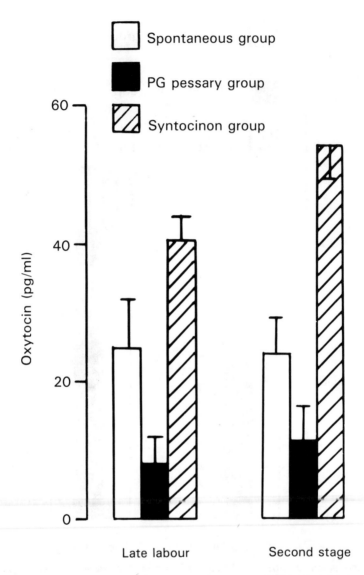

Figure 4. Comparison of plasma oxytocin levels (mean ± SEM) in late and second stage labour.

to hospital. Mean concentrations in late labour and second stage in these three groups are shown in Fig. 3. There is very little difference in the PGFM concentrations in late labour, whether induced or spontaneous. However, in the second stage, the group of patients who received Syntocinon had lower levels than the other two groups and significantly lower levels than patients in spontaneous labour ($p < 0.05$). This might suggest that Syntocinon is inhibiting prostaglandin production, which is contrary to the *in vitro* data of Fuchs *et al.* (1981).

In both late labour and second stage, oxytocin concentrations tended to be much lower in the prostaglandin pessary group, although none of these differences were significant (Fig. 4). These data suggest that administration of prostaglandins may inhibit oxytocin release. The fact that the oxytocin concentrations are so high in the

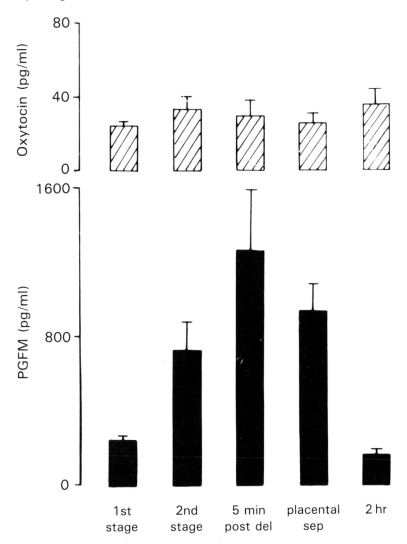

Figure 5. Plasma PGFM and oxytocin levels (mean ± SEM) during labour and in the immediate puerperium.

Syntocinon group probably reflects the fact that Syntocinon cross-reacts 100% with the oxytocin antiserum used in our assay. One might speculate that it is the combination of oxytocin and prostaglandins that is more important than the absolute levels of either hormone. Thus, with high oxytocin levels, less PGF might be required for labour and *vice versa*.

The role of oxytocin and prostaglandins in the third stage of labour has been investigated. PGFM and oxytocin concentrations were measured during the first and second stages of labour, 5 min after delivery, at placental separation and 2 h after delivery (Fig. 5). A dramatic increase in PGFM levels was demonstrated within 5 min of delivery before placental separation had occurred clinically and it may be that PGF is important for separation and expulsion of the placenta. There were no changes in oxytocin concentrations throughout the sampling time, suggesting that oxytocin is not involved in the third stage of labour.

References

Chard, T., Hudson, C. N., Edwards, C. R. W. and Boyd, N. R. H. (1971). Release of oxytocin and vasopressin by the human fetus during labour. *Nature (London)* **234**, 352.

Fuchs, A-R., Husslein, P. and Fuchs, F. (1981). Oxytocin and the initiation of human parturition. II Stimulation of prostaglandin production in human decidua by oxytocin. *American Journal of Obstetrics and Gynecology* **141**, 694.

Discussion

Dr Challis asked whether there was any evidence that the decidua itself might make oxytocin.

Dr Sellers said that she knew of none.

Dr Calder thought the explanation for the rapid rise in PGFM after insertion of a prostaglandin pessary might relate to the activity of 9-keto-reductase. Dr Murray Mitchell had recently suggested that this was an important mechanism. He wondered what evidence there was to suggest that PGE stimulated the myometrium.

Dr Keirse said that in his view 9-keto-reductase was not of major importance. The enzyme depended on NADP but in the cell the balance was heavily in favour of NADPH.

As to the effects of PGE, when injected into the myometrium it did indeed produce contractions.

Dr Calder agreed that this was the clinical observation, although studies had suggested that it might act as a myometrial relaxant. He wondered whether conversion to PGF might be necessary to bring about such a stimulation.

Dr Keirse said it was most unlikely that a sophisticated enzyme system switched PGE to PGF when the latter could be produced by a much simpler process.

General discussion

Dr Calder asked Panellists to speculate about the relative importance of PGE and PGF in labour.

Dr Husslein had studied levels of PGE and PGF metabolites in patients before labour, during early labour, at full dilatation, and then at intervals after delivery of the placenta. In general, much larger amounts of the F metabolite were found in the circulation than the E metabolite. The pre-post increase in the former was highly significant. In contrast, only 2 significant differences were found for the E metabolite, the first comparing all labour values together with control levels before labour, and the second comparing the 5 min post-partum value with all other values. He and other investigators had been surprised at how low values of the E metabolite were and he wondered what happened to the apparently large amounts of prostaglandin E synthesized, for example, under the pisseaktis stimulus. It was true that tremendous local changes would be required to be detected in the peripheral blood, but nonetheless there seemed no doubt that much more PGF was being synthesized and measured in the peripheral circulation than PGE at any time of parturition.

Dr Calder wondered if a conversion of PGE to PGF might explain this finding.

Dr Keirse said that he did not believe that PGF was more important than PGE. Under the influence of prostaglandin endoperoxide synthetase prostaglandin endoperoxides were produced. They could then be directed to the synthesis of prostacyclin or thromboxane or PGE. Quantities which were not required for any of these primary purposes would simply be converted to PGF, a process which did not seem to require any enzyme activity.

Dr Calder said that in clinical practice PGE given for any purpose was generally 5-10 times more potent than PGF.

Dr Husslein said that if one induced labour with PGE, one would only achieve vaginal delivery if PGF metabolite levels increased in the peripheral blood. At one time he believed that this meant induction with PGE was only possible if PGF synthesis were also stimulated. An alternative explanation, however, was that much of PGE administered was being transformed to PGF and perhaps neither was the most active agent.

Dr Challis said that the prostaglandin metabolism might be unimportant unless the relevant receptor populations were present. He wondered what information existed on PGE or PGF receptors.

Dr Keirse said that data from Kimball (1975), Crankshaw *et al.* (1979) and Bauknecht *et al.* (1981) had shown 2 different receptor populations, of which the E receptors with a high affinity appeared to be by far the more important. However, there was an additional explanation for Dr Husslein's finding that patients given PGE would only deliver if they had an increase in the PGF metabolite. It might be that such patients would only deliver if they were able to switch on the parturitional mechanism leading to the production of prostaglandin endoperoxides which could be converted into PGE, PGF or PGD.

Dr Calder wondered what purpose the synthesis of PGE in the amnion could serve. There seemed no biological need for it, if it were synthesized in the decidua.

Dr Challis said the critical question was whether amniotic PGE exerted its effects in the amnion itself or whether it crossed the chorion and entered the decidua. Personally he thought such transport was unlikely, but the question required investigation.

Dr Keirse doubted whether the prostaglandin poured into the liquor had any biological purpose whatever.

Dr MacKenzie asked for clarification of the opinions expressed by Dr Challis and Dr Kierse on prostaglandin levels through pregnancy. The former had suggested that they were rather static, the latter that they rose as pregnancy proceeded.

Dr Keirse said that the discussion related more precisely to how prostacyclin changed. Both of them agreed that it did not change dramatically during pregnancy. It then increased markedly early in labour, but showed little subsequent rise as labour proceeded. There seemed little evidence that it increased markedly during the last 4–5 weeks, although it was difficult to be certain since the levels of 6-keto $PGF_{1\alpha}$ which had been reported in pregnancy seemed artificially high.

Dr Challis agreed that some earlier reported levels of 6-keto $PGF_{1\alpha}$ seemed to suffer from measurement problems. There was, however, more recent data showing a tendency for it to increase in amniotic fluid.

As to the rise during pregnancy, the increase in PGI was less than that in PGE plus PGF and so the net result was an increase in stimulatory activity. The question of whether PGE and PGF rose throughout pregnancy was more difficult. Data on the urinary metabolite of PGF suggested that they did, though very slowly.

Dr Husslein had not made serial determinations throughout pregnancy but had compared 4 groups of patients, those in terminal labour, term early labour, preterm labour and a comparable group at preterm with no contractions. Contrary to findings in the United States, they found the preterm no labour group had lower values than the terminal labour group, and within the preterm group as a whole those with contractions had a significant rise over those with no contractions. Earlier data also suggested that preterm labour patients also had higher prostaglandin metabolite levels.

Dr Calder said that their main interest was what happened during the phase when the patient was about to go into labour. It was a difficult subject to investigate but he wondered whether there were any prostaglandin measurements that might predict the onset of preterm or term labour.

Dr Keirse said that in an attempt to establish the synthetic marker they were studying the production of 6-keto $PGF_{1\alpha}$. It had the advantage of being excreted in the urine and metabolized via beta oxidation. An increase in the levels of this substance might reflect endoperoxide changes, but so far the technical problems in its determination were considerable.

Dr Husslein said that attempts were being made to distinguish 'real preterm' from 'false preterm' labour on the basis of circulating PGF metabolite levels. If a radioimmunoassay were available that were sufficiently rapid it could perhaps be incorporated into clinical practice.

Dr Murray wondered whether Dr Husslein had looked at the activity of prostaglandin synthetase in decidual samples from patients undergoing elective caesarean section and those whose sections were for obstructed labour.

Dr Husslein said that he had found higher basal production levels of PGF in the decidua of the active labour group. However, the oxytocin effect was demonstrable in both groups. Other workers had found the decidua in labour to produce low levels of prostaglandin which they attributed to a depletion of arachidonic acid. In his own data, however, the results of oxytocin stimulation were similar for both spontaneous labour and elective caesarean section, but decidua from the spontaneous labour group produced more PGF than those from the elective sections.

Dr Keirse wondered how decidual tissue had been obtained.

Dr Husslein said that it was scraped from the inside of the myometrium. The tissue was divided into 3 and used for receptor determination, *in vitro* assay and histological study, the latter to ensure that pure decidual tissue had been obtained.

Dr Challis said that his decidual specimens were scraped from the chorion.

References

Bauknecht, T., Krahe, B., Rechenbach, U., Zahradnik, H. P. and Breckwoldt, M. (1981). Distribution of prostaglandin E_2 and prostaglandin $F_{2\alpha}$ receptors in human myometrium. *Acta Endocrinologica* **98**, 446.

Crankshaw, D. J., Crankshaw, J., Branda, L. A. and Daniel, E. E. (1979). Receptors for E type prostaglandins in the plasma membrane of nonpregnant human myometrium. *Archives of Biochemistry and Biophysics* **198**, 70.

Kimball, F. A., Kirton, K. T., Spilman, C. H. and Wyngarden, L. J. (1975). Prostaglandin E_1 specific binding in human myometrium. *Biology of Reproduction* **13**, 482.

Prostaglandins and induction of labour: present dilemmas

I. Z. MacKENZIE

Nuffield Department of Obstetrics and Gynaecology,
John Radcliffe Hospital, Headington, Oxford, UK

It is now more than 15 years since prostaglandins (PGs) became available to clinicians to assist in the management of labour induction at term. When considering the progress in the development of prostaglandins for this purpose, I believe the story has unfolded in 3 basic chapters. During the first 5 years, wild enthusiastic efforts were made, exploring many possible uses and administration routes, with some resulting disenchantment. The second 5 years was a period of reflection and reappraisal, more precisely of just what advantages the prostaglandins had to offer the clinical obstetrician. During the past 5 years a consolidation of knowledge has taken place, reinforcing the role that PGs have in labour induction which has inevitably resulted in more questions and uncertainties. It is the fine tuning that requires attention and this and following presentations are aimed at addressing some of these present problems and hopefully providing ideas for improvements in clinical management.

Development of PGs in labour induction

During the first 5 years considerable effort was directed to researching different methods of giving prostaglandins, assessing dosage requirements for the 2 natural prostaglandins, PGE_2 and $PGF_{2\alpha}$ and exploring possible clinical roles. The findings of these initial 5 years of investigation were that local administration required lower dosages than oral or intravenous administration and that gastrointestinal side-effects which occur with the other routes, were much less troublesome with intra-uterine administration. Vaginal administration was, however, similar to oral or intravenous use and all 3 were considered untenable routes. In the UK, PGE_2 was preferred to $PGF_{2\alpha}$, since gastrointestinal side-effects were less common but $PGF_{2\alpha}$ found greater favour in the US, South Africa, Australia and most other countries. The application of prostaglandins for pregnancy termination soon became established and has largely sustained its popularity for the management of second trimester abortion, at least in the UK. However, most studies assessing the place of PGs in labour induction

The role of prostaglandins in labour, edited by Clive Wood, 1985: Royal Society of Medicine Services International Congress and Symposium Series No. 92, published by Royal Society of Medicine Services Limited.

failed to show any advantage over oxytocin but found that vomiting and diarrhoea accompanied intravenous infusions. For this reason, the PGs fell from favour.

During the second 5 year period interest was renewed, following the work of Andrew Calder in collaboration with Mostyn Embrey, one of the pioneers of the study of the clinical applications of prostaglandins. They showed that these agents appeared to be particularly effective in inducing labour when the cervix was unripe and the process would be expected to be difficult. In so doing, PGs could enhance the prospects for induced labour, so reducing the high rate of morbidity commonly associated with such labour inductions. Mostyn Embrey had shown as early as 1969 that intravenous PGE_2 was more effective for such inductions than intravenous oxytocin (Embrey 1969). However, vomiting and diarrhoea were a problem and their efforts were directed to exploring extra-amniotic administration of prostaglandins using a continuous infusion through an indwelling, transcervical Foley catheter. They achieved some considerable success (Calder *et al.* 1974).

The inevitable next stage in development was the concept of pre-treatment of the cervix by administration of a small dose of prostaglandin on a single occasion by extra-amniotic instillation, with subsequent labour induction planned 12–24 h later (Calder *et al.* 1977). Though effective, the method has certain disadvantages in that aseptic precautions are essential to avoid introducing infection into the uterus. The technique also requires the use of the lithotomy position and is an invasive procedure which by the end of the 1970s was against 'public' wishes. As a consequence the vaginal route was then explored and broadly similar results were obtained with a much simpler approach.

The observation that many patients proceeded into labour in an apparently spontaneous manner had obvious attractions to patients and staff alike. The technique of vaginal PG administration was explored in those patients in whom induction was expected to be simple, and the current vogue for routine labour induction using vaginal prostaglandins arose from these intial studies (MacKenzie and Embrey 1978). With the continued demand from women for a much more conservative approach to labour induction, the instillation of prostaglandins by the vaginal route or by oral ingestion was more readily acceptable than the hitherto conventional induction techniques of low amniotomy and intravenous oxytocin titration. For some reason however, the oral route has not been attractive and has certainly not been generally favoured by obstetricians.

During the most recent 5 year period the thoughts of clinicians studying the use of prostaglandins for labour induction have tended to polarize upon more specific problems, the principle having been generally accepted that locally administered PGs produce the most impressive results for labour induction whether the cervix is ripe or unripe. With most innovative ideas the overwhelming enthusiasm that accompanies the initial discovery is followed by a period of disenchantment, after which a lower level of general acceptance continues unless the technique is ultimately abandoned. Surprisingly, locally-administered prostaglandin for labour induction has not, as yet, fallen from grace and remains attractive both to obstetricians and their patients. However, many uncertainties have been brought to light during the past 5 years.

Current uncertainties

Firstly, one should give brief consideration to the most appropriate route to administer prostaglandins. I think most of the information currently available indicates that oral preparations for routine labour induction are perfectly satisfactory, providing the cervix is favourable and particularly if the patient is multiparous. This route, however, would not appear very suitable for cervical priming, due to the need for prolonged treatment and the side-effects encountered with the required doses. Virtually all the current information indicates that locally administered prostaglandins offers a very effective way of inducing labour and, in most instances, ripening the cervix when it is particularly unfavourable. But are the results of vaginal instillation as effective as extra-amniotic instillation? Of particular importance to the issue concerning the site of treatment is the issue of the mode of action of prostaglandins when given locally. Is their effect upon the cervix direct, modifying cervical form and function, or an effect mediated through myometrial stimulation and uterine contractions? If it is the former, as Dr Ledger's work on the sheep implies, then the approach developed by some Scandinavian units of endocervical application and considered by Professor Keirse at this Meeting, is the most logical technique so far considered (Wingerup *et al.* 1979). However, I have some doubts over the precision of intra-cervical canal instillations of prostaglandins. The skill required to ensure correct placement detracts somewhat from the principle of providing a simple method for labour induction.

Fundamental to the discussions of vaginal administration is the problem that all of us who deal with patients have had to face: there has either been no commercial preparation available for clinical use or those that have been provided have not always been found to be satisfactory. This has led to a number of makeshift preparations including viscous cellulose gels, wax-based pessaries and the administration of tablets originally prepared for oral ingestion, together with non-biodegradable polymer pessaries such as those studied by Embrey *et al.* (1980). The recently developed triacetin gel released by Upjohn and undergoing clinical trials provides some optimism for the future. However, while the initial results I hope will show good cause for this optimism, we still need to address the other uncertainties that have been noted in recent years.

Among them is the question of whether PGE_2 is the most appropriate prostaglandin to use. Our own studies in Oxford (MacKenzie *et al.* 1979) and those of Neilson *et al.* (1983) both suggest that PGE_2 is superior to $PGF_{2\alpha}$ for ripening the unfavourable cervix. But is this also the case for routine labour induction, since $PGF_{2\alpha}$ would appear to be the more important endogenous PG, with increasing concentrations found in liquor and blood with advancing labour? In contrast to our observations, MacLennan and Green (1979) in Australia reported effective ripening with $PGF_{2\alpha}$. However, their observations were not well controlled and tended to include patients of varying parity and all shades of cervical favourability. Whether one prostaglandin is better than another can be debated, but virtually all studies assessing efficacy have concluded that successful cervical ripening will not be achieved in all patients and that labour outcome is not universally successful, irrespective of the route of administration or the PG used. It is therefore possible that an analogue might be developed with more specific actions upon cervical morphology and function. It could have considerable advantages if the effect upon cervical priming could be increased and such effects achieved by a direct cervical action rather than inducing myometrial contractions. To some extent this can be achieved with the administration of oestradiol but such treatment, although improving the cervical state, has much less effect upon labour outcome. It appears therefore that some effect upon myometrial activity is possibly desirable.

One further, no less fundamental issue is to decide whether induction regimens, of which a large number have been described in the literature, should be developed with two separate concepts in mind:— pre-induction cervical ripening and routine simple induction. The programme of the present Meeting implies that we currently consider the two types of cervical condition as separate clinical problems.

While I personally endorse this approach, I believe it could be reasonably argued that the distinction between the unfavourable and favourable cervix is very blurred, and a single evolving protocol might be better. Among the clinical considerations which to some extent dictate a preference is the question of safety. If treatment protocols are similar for cervical ripening and labour induction then the theoretical or genuine risks to the foetus must be the same. Indeed how great a risk to the foetus is the local administration of prostaglandins? There have been sporadic reports in the literature of foetal compromise following prostaglandin administration for both ripening and routine induction and this has led to a view that all patients given prostaglandins should have continuous foetal surveillance from that time until delivery. This can inevitably pose logistic problems in those patients with a very unfavourable cervix in whom ripening and labour can last for many hours.

Amongst the issues perhaps causing the greatest concern to clinicians is the apparent lack of predictability of uterine response to locally administered prostaglandins. My own analysis of the literature some years ago, comparing uterine over-stimulation or hypertonus following prostaglandin administration to that observed following spontaneous labour or labour induced with intravenous oxytocin, concluded that the incidence of this hazard was similar with both oxytocin and prostaglandins-induced labour and was similar to the incidence following spontaneous onset of labour. Although an infrequent problem, it can have dire consequences for both mother and foetus.

It has long been recognized that the measurement of the natural prostaglandins in peripheral blood is unreliable and is thought to give an inaccurate picture of endogenous prostaglandin production or exogenous PG kinetics. It is only in the last few years, with the discovery of an apparently reliable bicyclo-PGE metabolite to study prostaglandin levels in the peripheral circulation following exogenous administration, that kinetic studies have been feasible. With the advent of this bicyclo-PGEM assay it has now become possible to observe the release and absorption of prostaglandins from various vehicles and, at least in theory, to tailor the release profiles according to the required result. Dr Sellars will present some of the results we have obtained in our Department in Oxford, examining various release profiles and attempting to equate PG levels in maternal circulation with cervical improvement and subsequent labour outcome. The information currently available is limited and I recognize that it is also at variance with the results obtained by others.

Whether we can make significant progress remains to be seen. The uncertainties and problems exist however, and efforts must be made to resolve them.

References

Calder, A. A., Embrey, M. P. and Hillier, K. (1974). Extraamniotic prostaglandin E$_2$ for induction of labour at term. *British Journal of Obstetrics and Gynaecology* **81**, 39.

Calder, A. A., Embrey, M. P. and Tait, T. (1977). Ripening of the cervix with extraamniotic prostaglandin E$_2$ in viscous gel before induction of labour. *British Journal of Obstetrics and Gynaecology* **84**, 264.

Embrey, M. P. (1969). The effect of prostaglandins on the human pregnant uterus. *Journal of Obstetrics and Gynaecology of the British Commonwealth* **76**, 783.

Embrey, M. P., Graham, N. B. and McNeill, M. E. (1980). Introduction of labour with a sustained release prostaglandin E$_2$ vaginal pessary. *British Medical Journal* **281**, 901.

Mackenzie, I. Z. and Embrey, M. P. (1978). The influence of pre-induction vaginal prostaglandin E_2 gel upon subsequent labour outcome. *British Journal of Obstetrics and Gynaecology* **85**, 657.

Mackenzie, I. Z. and Embrey, M .P. (1979). A comparison of PGE_2 and $PGF_{2\alpha}$ vaginal gel for ripening the cervix before induction of labour. *British Journal of Obstetrics and Gynaecology* **86**, 167.

MacLennan, A. H. and Green, R. C. (1979). Cervical ripening and induction of labour with intravaginal prostaglandin $F_{2\alpha}$. *Lancet* **1**, 117.

Neilson, D. R., Prins, R. P., Bolton, R. N., Mark, C. and Watson, P. (1983). A comparison of prostaglandin E_2 gel and prostaglandin $F_{2\alpha}$ gel for preinduction cervical ripening. *American Journal of Obstetrics and Gynecology* **146**, 526.

Wingerup, L., Anderson, K.-E. and Ulmsten, U. (1979). Ripening the cervix and induction of labour in patients at term by single intracervical application of prostaglandin E_2 in viscous gel. *Acta Obstetrica Gynaecologica Scandinavica* Suppl. **84**, 15.

High Bishop score and labour induction[*]

A. CAMERON

Department of Obstetrics and Gynaecology,
Royal Infirmary, Glasgow, UK

Improvements in the techniques of labour induction are constantly being sought, but the efficacy of intravenous oxytocin and amniotomy means that it is probably the most common method of labour induction. Prostaglandin E_2 (PGE_2) either in oral or vaginal tablet form, has been widely used for induction of labour and is registered for this use in the United Kingdom and other countries. Several reports have described the use of extemporaneous preparations of PGE_2 in gel for ripening the unfavourable cervix and inducing labour, but such preparations are of uncertain stability (Calder 1977, MacKenzie 1978, O'Herlihy 1979, Wingerup 1979). A stable preparation of PGE_2 in a triacetin gel base has now been developed by Upjohn Ltd.

The preparation used in the present study was PGE_2 at a dosage of 1 or 2 mg in a triacetin gel base in a pre-filled syringe. A randomized open-label trial compared the effects of 1–3 mg of PGE_2 gel with those of intravenous oxytocin for the induction of patients at 38 weeks or more gestation and with a Bishop score of 5 or more. The randomization procedure was arranged such that more patients received PGE_2 gel than oxytocin, since our main purpose was to study the new preparation.

Table 1

Comparison of intravenous oxytocin with vaginal PGE_2 gel

283 patients	Cervical score >5
Random allocation	
Amniotomy plus immediate intravenous oxytocin titration 1–32 mU/min	1,2 or 3 mg of PGE_2 vaginal gel plus amniotomy when in labour

[*]This trial represents a multicentre randomized comparison of PGE_2 vaginal gel against amniotomy and intravenous oxytocin in favourable induction. Participating centres: Northern General Hospital, Sheffield (P. Stewart); Withington Hospital, Manchester (M. D. Read); Redhill District Hospital, Surrey (A. Gordon-Wright); Simpson Memorial Hospital, Edinburgh (F. D. Johnstone); Arrowe Park Hospital, Wirral (D. H. Darwich); St Mary's Hospital, Portsmouth (A. D. Clarke); Royal Maternity Hospital, Glasgow (A. A. Calder).

The role of prostaglandins in labour, edited by Clive Wood, 1985: Royal Society of Medicine Services International Congress and Symposium Series No. 92, published by Royal Society of Medicine Services Limited.

Table 2

Bishop scores for assessing the favourability of the cervix

Score	0	1	2	3
Dilatation (cm)	0	1–2	3–4	5+
Effacement (per cent)	0–30	40–50	60–70	80+
Station	−3	−2	−1/0	+1+
Consistency	Firm	Med	Soft	
Position	Posterior	Mid	Anterior	

Table 3

Exclusion criteria

Patients with a known hypersensitivity to prostaglandins

Patients with a history of asthma, glaucoma or raised intra-ocular pressure

Patients with obstetrical conditions which contraindicate labour or vaginal delivery

Patients with ruptured membranes

Patients in labour or who have a previous labour induction attempt during this pregnancy

Patients who have had a previous caesarean section or hysterotomy

Patients with a history of precipitate delivery

Patients were randomly allocated into a group who had labour induced by amniotomy and immediate intravenous oxytocin at an escalating rate of 1–32 mU/min to establish labour, and a group who had labour induced with PGE_2 vaginal gel followed by amniotomy when they were in established labour (Table 1). The original Bishop score (Table 2) was used to assess the favourability of the cervix (Bishop 1964). The exclusion criteria are listed in Table 3.

Methods

All patients received 1 mg of PGE_2 inserted high vaginally. They were then monitored with external cardiotocography and 6 h later were reassessed by the same observer. Amniotomy was performed if patients were in labour and the cervix had dilated at least 2 cm. Patients who were having some contractions and were thought to be in early labour were given a further dose of 1 mg of PGE_2. Those patients who were not having regular uterine contractions and whose cervical dilatations had not increased by at least 2 cm were given a dose of 2 mg of PGE_2. Artificial rupture of membranes were performed for patients in both of these latter 2 groups who became established in labour before 12 h. All patients had formal amniotomy at 12 h if it had not already been performed.

Results

For the purpose of this study, a successful case was one in which an increase in cervical dilatation of 3 cm was achieved within 12 h. Of 298 cases who were enrolled, 283 were evaluable. They consisted of 121 primigravidae, of whom 74 received gel and

47 oxytocin. There were 162 multigravid patients, of whom 103 received gel and 59 oxytocin. The ages of the patients in the primigravid group and the multigravid group were comparable, as was the distribution of the number of previous deliveries in the multigravid group. Very few patients were more than gravida 3. The most common reasons for induction in both groups were suspected postmaturity, mild to moderate hypertension or foetal growth retardation (Table 4). The baseline Bishop scores for both primigravidae and multigravidae were similar in the gel and oxytocin groups. The ranges were also very similar (Table 5).

Table 4
Reason for induction of labour

	Primigravidae		Multigravidae	
Hypertension	23	20	15	10
Post dates	34	18	51	26
Intrauterine growth retardation	2	2	22	8
Other	15	7	15	15
	74	47	103	59

Table 5
Baseline Bishop scores

	Primigravidae		Multigravidae	
	Gel	Oxytocin	Gel	Oxytocin
Mean	6·85	6·87	6·61	6·9
Range	5–11	5–10	5–12	5–11

The overall success rate was higher in the multigravid patients, with 68 per cent having a successful induction of labour with only 1 mg of PGE_2, whereas fewer than half the primigravid group had a successful outcome with that dosage (Table 6). For patients who were regarded as failures, it is clear that no patient failed with only 1 mg of PGE_2 and that the majority of patients in both groups who were regarded as failures had received 3 mg of PGE_2.

In both the primigravidae and multigravidae the gel-treated group had a significantly longer induction to delivery interval. This has previously been reported by Kennedy *et al.* (1962) using vaginal prostaglandin tablets in multigravid patients with favourable induction features. In contrast, the amniotomy to delivery interval (Table 7) showed significant differences between the gel-treated and oxytocin groups, both in the primigravidae and multigravidae. The mean times for the gel-treated subjects, especially the multigravidae, were very short, some patients delivering almost immediately after amniotomy was performed. A peculiar finding was a significant shortening of the second stage in multigravidae who received prostaglandin gel. This was not the case in the primigravid group who had similar mean second stages to the oxytocin group. The modes of delivery were similar in all groups.

There were no differences in the Apgar scores at 1 min or 5 min between the gel and oxytocin groups in either primigravidae or multigravidae. An important finding was that in the primigravidae induced with oxytocin there was a higher incidence of primary post-partum haemorrhage than in the corresponding gel-induced group. Similar observations have been reported by Brinsden and Clark (1978) and by MacKenzie (1979).

Table 6

Dose of PGE$_2$ gel used and success rate

Dose (mg)	Success Primigravidae	Multigravidae	Failure Primigravidae	Multigravidae
1	27 (48)[a]	67 (68)	0 (0)	0 (0)
2	5 (9)	4 (4)	5 (28)	2 (40)
3	24 (43)	27 (27)	13 (72)	3 (60)

[a] Figures in brackets are percentages

Table 7

Amniotomy to delivery interval (h)

	Primigravidae Gel	Oxytocin	Multigravidae Gel	Oxytocin
Mean	$4 \cdot 5 \pm 2 \cdot 4$[a]	$7 \cdot 9 \pm 3 \cdot 2$	$2 \cdot 0 \pm 1 \cdot 8$[a]	$5 \cdot 7 \pm 2 \cdot 2$
Range	$0 \cdot 8 - 11 \cdot 0$	$3 \cdot 4 - 18 \cdot 0$	$0 \cdot 0 - 9 \cdot 2$	$2 \cdot 0 - 11 \cdot 6$

[a] $p < 0 \cdot 001$

In conclusion, this study confirms that PGE$_2$ in gel form is a suitable agent for induction of labour in patients with a favourable cervix and that the new gel formulation is well suited to this purpose. The dosage stipulated in the protocol for this study was clearly inadequate for most primigravid subjects but the results for the multigravidae were very encouraging. Some obstetricians might be concerned about the very short second stages in some of the multiparae, but this has not been a feature of similar previous studies and may have been a chance finding. Vaginal administration of prostaglandins in gel has already proved highly popular with patients and obstetricians alike, as witnessed by the enthusiasm shown for 'home made' preparations. The new formulation at last provides clinicians with a purpose-prepared vaginal prostaglandin gel.

Further work is now required to establish the appropriate dose regimes for different types of induction.

References

Bishop, E. H. (1964). Pelvic scoring for elective induction. *Obstetrics and Gynecology* **24**, 266.

Brinsden, P. S. and Clark, A. D. (1978). Postpartum haemorrhage after induced and spontaneous labour. *British Medical Journal* **2**, 855.

Calder, A. A., Embrey, M. P. and Tait, T. (1977). Ripening of the cervix with extraamniotic prostaglandin E$_2$ in viscous gel before induction of labour. *British Journal of Obstetrics and Gynaecology* **84**, 264.

Kennedy, J. H., Stewart, P., Barlow, D. H., Hulan, E. H. and Calder, A. A. (1982). Induction of labour: a comparison of a single prostaglandin E$_2$ vaginal tablet with amniotomy and intravenous oxytocin. *British Journal of Obstetrics and Gynaecology* **89**, 704.

MacKenzie, I. Z. (1979). Induction of labour and postpartum haemorrhage. *British Medical Journal* **1**, 750.

MacKenzie, I. Z. and Embrey, M. P. (1978). The influence of pre-induction vaginal prostaglandin E$_2$ gel upon subsequent labour. *British Journal of Obstetrics and Gynaecology* **85**, 657.

O'Herlihy, C. and MacDonald, H. N. (1979). Influence of preinduction prostaglandin E_2 vaginal gel on cervical ripening and labour. *Obstetrics and Gynecology* **54**, 708.
Wingerup, L., Andersson, K. E. and Ulmsten, U. (1979). Ripening of the cervix and induction of labour in patients at term by single intracervical application of prostaglandin E_2 in viscous gel. *Acta Obstetrica Gynaecologica Scandinavica* (Suppl. 84), 11.

Discussion

Dr MacKenzie wondered how statistically sound it was to place more patients in one group than another. In addition, because of the blocking design, it was conceivable that one centre could have treated all the prostaglandin and another all the oxytocin patients.

Dr Hinchley said that they had altered the randomization half-way through the study, to produce a 2:1 design. While statistically this was not fully legitimate, it had been dictated by practical considerations. The drug regulatory authority was more interested in the safety and efficacy of the compound than the standard.

As to the block design, it was conceivable that different centres might have had disproportionate concentrations of prostaglandin or oxytocin patients. In fact that had not happened.

Dr MacKenzie wondered whether some patients had had 3 treatments and how many had required oxytocin.

Dr Cameron said that the protocol called for repeated treatment after 6 h and reassessment a further 6 h later unless labour was established by then. Patients having had 2 treatments who were then established in labour had amniotomy. Those not established in labour by 12 h also had an amniotomy and were counted as failures. None, however, received 3 treatments, though some received 3 mg (1 mg plus 2 mg) of PGE_2. As to the oxytocin requirement, of 14 primigravid patients treated with the gel, 10 ultimately required oxytocin.

Dr Murray wondered how many successes also required augmentation with oxytocin to maintain their progress. If the definition of success was 3 cm dilatation a patient could still require augmentation after this dilatation was reached.

Dr Hinchley said that some patients progressed to what was technically success but then required caesarean section, but none of the technical successes required oxytocin.

Dr Keirse noted that in the primigravid patients the average second stage was over 70 min in both groups, which he regarded as long. He wondered if it was counted from full dilatation, irrespective of whether the patient was pushing or not.

Dr Cameron said that the definition would depend on each labour ward, but in his unit full dilatation was diagnosed when the vertex was visible. He did not believe that 70 min was an excessively long second stage. Many of the patients had epidural blocks, following which second stages of over an hour were not uncommon.

Dr Calder said that attitudes to the second stage were changing and in a recent study the longest second stage recorded in a primigravida was 5·5 h.

Dr Husslein said that before concluding that prostaglandin gel was not as efficient as oxytocin for the high Bishop score patients, one had to look critically at the question of dosage. A dose of 1 mg was certainly low, and he wondered how often hyperstimulation was seen at a dose of 2 mg. In addition, early amniotomy would favour the oxytocin group, which would influence the comparison.

Dr Cameron said that 5 cases of hypertonus had been recorded, though none in his patients.

Dr Read said that 2 primigravid patients whom he had treated had shown hypertonus after an initial dose of 1 mg which had precluded them receiving a second dose. The hypertonus settled without problems and they progressed to a normal vaginal delivery.

Dr Murray said the same was true for a primigravid patient in his series.

Dr Husslein had observed similar phenomena with the 3 mg vaginal tablet but the problem had either subsided or was dealt with by a β-mimetic agent. So while hyperstimulation was of some concern it should not be over-emphasized. It also occurred with oxytocin.

Dr MacKenzie thought it appropriate to distinguish between hypertonus and hyperstimulation. A hypertonic contraction was a sustained contraction.

Dr Read said that both his cases occurred during the first hour, while patients were on continuous external monitoring and the contractions were sustained in both cases.

Dr Murray said that his case was not a classic hypertonus. Rather than being sustained and prolonged, the patient had frequent systolic contractions. However, they were sufficient to induce foetal bradycardia, and hypertonus was defined from its effects on the foetal circulation.

Dr Stewart said that when they had compared the vaginal tablet with oxytocin there was far less need for analgesia in the prostaglandin compared to the oxytocin group.

Dr Cameron said that his impression was similar, though he had no detailed figures. He confirmed that they had performed the same number of vaginal examinations on patients in both groups.

Dr Gordon-Wright wondered whether those rapid labours that had occurred in the multiparous patients, particularly the precipitous second stages, had been regarded as hazardous.

Dr Cameron said that they had sometimes been alarming, both for the women and for the midwives.

Dr Gordon-Wright asked how such a situation might be avoided. He wondered if the most rapidly delivering patients had the most favourable cervices.

Dr Cameron said that he thought that they had. They were also among the most highly parous patients.

Dr Calder said that closer examination of these labours might be appropriate. He wondered whether the short second stage reflected more efficient uterine contractility.

Dr MacKenzie said that in his experience of vaginal prostaglandins a short second stage nearly always followed a short first stage.

Dr Taylor wondered how patients had reacted to the various types of induction. In Edinburgh, patients receiving gel, who were warned in advance that the onset of labour might be delayed, accepted the method very well. In the absence of such a warning, however, they tended to become agitated.

Dr Cameron said that in general patient acceptability was fairly high. Some patients were a little concerned that others were delivering sooner than they, but since they were able to get up and move about they were generally happy with the method. In the study of Kennedy *et al.* (1982) 90 per cent of patients who received the Prostin™ vaginal tablet had expressed complete satisfaction, compared to a much lower acceptance rate of intravenous oxytocin.

Dr Husslein said that in measuring the length of labour it was vital to examine the type of analgesia employed. When they had given pethedine to patients with good contractions they had dramatically shortened the first and second stages. In contrast, an epidural block might have a less marked effect.

Dr Keirse wondered whether, with the 1 mg dose, it might be preferable to start at 3.00 a.m. so that the 12 h assessment occurred at 3.00 p.m. If the onset were slow, then this early period might be better timed at night than in the morning.

Dr Cameron thought that for multiparous patients 9.00 a.m. was an appropriate start, since most of them did deliver with 1 mg. With primiparous patients it might be more appropriate to change the dosage than to start very early in the morning, which he did not regard as appropriate.

Dr Walton said that his group were finding 12–15 h induction–delivery intervals from the prostaglandin tablets. Giving such tablets at 6.00 a.m. produced a large number of night deliveries, so much so that they were considering changing to 6.00 p.m., at least for primiparous patients, so that they would deliver during the daytime.

Dr Murray said that he would be reluctant to alter the 6.00 a.m. starting time. Some of his colleagues gave the tablets at 9.00 p.m. but those patients (particularly primigravidae) who failed to go into labour had a disturbed night with contractions and then faced a day of labour in an already demoralized state. Such a change was therefore undesirable.

Prostaglandins in the difficult induction

P. STEWART

Department of Obstetrics and Gynaecology,
Northern General Hospital, Sheffield, UK

When the cervix is ripe in a multigravid woman a successful outcome is almost assured when induction of labour is planned by the clinician. The question of whether or not an induction will succeed has now been replaced with the question of which method to use. Most methods are equally effective and the final decision may be determined by maternal preference (Kennedy *et al.* 1982). Cameron's data (this Symposium) confirm these earlier findings. There are, however, certain circumstances in which the obstetrician can be less certain of the outcome of the intervention. They include a women with an unripe cervix, with previous uterine surgery, with a high presenting part or ruptured membranes and with no sign of the onset of spontaneous contractions. An unripe cervix is often a common feature of these situations.

Intravenous infusion of oxytocin, together with fore-water amniotomy is still a very widely used method of induction. It does, however, require an intravenous infusion and therefore tends to restrict the woman's movement during labour. The amniotomy itself, with its consequent release of endogenous prostaglandins (Mitchell *et al.* 1977) appears to be an essential part of this approach, but when the cervix is unripe, patients may find the procedure unacceptable (Stewart 1977). Calder and Embrey (1975) also found that this method of induction in women with an unripe cervix was likely to lead to prolonged labour and a poor outcome for both mother and baby.

Such findings have therefore prompted attempts to ripen the cervix prior to the induction of labour. Many methods have been used. Ezimokhai and Nwambineli (1980) employed a simple extra-amniotic Foley catheter and Lackritz *et al.* (1979) used an intra-cervical laminarium. Such mechanical methods may produce their effect by the release of local prostaglandins, but there is some evidence (Nicolaides *et al.* 1983) that this may not be the case when intra-cervical Lamicel, a hydrophilic polymer impregnated with magnesium sulphate, is used. Such mechanical means can achieve cervical ripening, but they are necessarily invasive and in general take longer than pharmacological agents to produce their effects.

Among pharmacological approaches, oxytocin (Valentine 1977) and dehydro-epiandrosterone sulphate (Mochizuki and Tojo 1980) have proved of little value. Local application of oestradiol has a ripening action (Gordon and Calder 1977), and further

The role of prostaglandins in labour, edited by Clive Wood, 1985: Royal Society of Medicine Services International Congress and Symposium Series No. 92, published by Royal Society of Medicine Services Limited.

studies of the effects of relaxin are needed before any firm conclusions can be made regarding its use (McLennan et al. 1980). The work of Calder et al. (1977) using a single application of 240–480 μg of prostaglandin E_2 (PGE$_2$) in an aqueous methylhydroxyethyl-cellulose (tylose) gel prior to surgical induction established the value of the natural prostaglandins for cervical ripening. MacKenzie and Embrey (1977) have shown the vaginal route is equally effective. However, many problems still remain with the use of these agents.

One of these is the uncertainty of action of PGE$_2$ when given by the extra-amniotic or vaginal route in a tylose gel. Approximately 50 per cent of primigravidae will go into labour following initial ripening treatment alone. The proportion is much higher in multigravidae. Although the ideal ripening agent would affect the cervix without producing uterine activity, as the ultimate object of pre-treatment of the cervix is to enable successful induction of labour this action of PGE$_2$, although perhaps inconvenient, cannot be considered as a major disadvantage. It may often preclude the need for formal induction. It could, however, be a problem in 'high risk' pregnancies. All patients receiving this treatment should have careful foetal monitoring in order to detect any foetal distress should labour ensue (Stewart and Calder 1981).

This effect of PGE$_2$ on the myometrium is not seen when oestradiol is used as a ripening agent. In a comparative study of 60 primigravidae using 450 μg of PGE$_2$ and 150 mg of oestradiol administered extra-amniotically via a Foley catheter, both agents had an equal effect on the cervix (Stewart et al. 1981). As expected, half the PGE$_2$ group did become established in labour without requiring a formal induction and there were no predictive factors to indicate which women would respond in this way. The final outcome was, however, poorer in the oestradiol group. There were 9 caesarean sections among these patients compared to 3 in the PGE$_2$ group of which 4 were carried out for failure to progress in labour with no evidence of cephalo-pelvic disproportion. Tromans et al. (1981) in a similar study, though using the vaginal route in patients of mixed parity obtained similar results, with a high incidence of lower segment caesarean sections performed because of failure to progress in their oestradiol group. The unripe cervix may point to a biological defect, not only in the cervix itself, but also of uterine function. PGE$_2$ may be able to overcome this defect, both of the cervix and the myometrium, but oestradiol cannot. For this reason PGE$_2$ appears to have an advantage over oestradiol as a ripening agent.

Early work with PGE$_2$ gels suggested that there was little to choose between the extra-amniotic and vaginal routes as methods of administering the drug. The former route is more invasive, but enables a very low dose to be used with a minimal chance of side-effects. The latter is more convenient, but requires a higher dosage. Any comparisons have been bedevilled by the lack of standard preparations of PGE$_2$. The introduction of a commercial vaginal tablet has provided a formulation of uniform concentration and predictable stability. As a result, some standardization of management has become possible.

Study I

We have compared the efficacy of such a tablet with that of 450 μg of PGE$_2$ in tylose gel delivered by the extra-amniotic route, in a randomized study of 62 primigravidae, all with an unfavourable cervix (Stewart et al. 1983). All patients had a singleton pregnancy with a cephalic presentation and a cervical score $\leqslant 4$. They were randomized into 2 groups, both having their treatment commenced at 15.00 h on the day prior to that on which formal induction was planned. In Group I, 450 μg of PGE$_2$ in a tylose gel was delivered into the extra-amniotic space using a Foley catheter. If labour did not ensue, an amniotomy with intravenous oxytocin was commenced at 09.00 the next morning. In Group II, the initial treatment was with a 3 mg PGE_2 vaginal tablet which was repeated at 09.00 the next morning and also at 15.00 h on the second day if necessary.

The results for patients in Group I are given in Fig. 1 (left). Seventeen of the 32 patients went into labour after treatment with PGE_2 alone, although 7 of them did require oxytocin for augmentation later in labour. The mean duration of the first stage of labour among all Group I patients was 9.3 h. The results of treatment of the 30 patients in Group II are given in Fig. 1 (right). Four patients failed to go into labour after receiving 3 PGE_2 vaginal tablets and of those who did labour, 13 required oxytocin infusions to augment their labour once it had been induced. The mean duration of the first stage was 9·2 h.

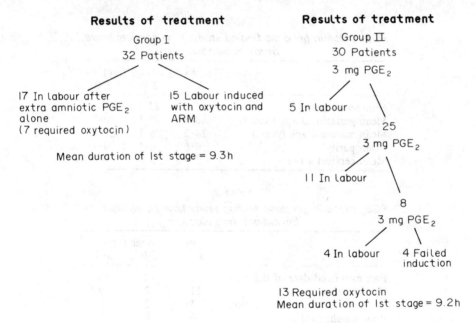

Figure 1. Comparison of extra-amniotic PGE_2 (Group I, left) with vaginal administration (Group II, right) in the induction of labour in patients with cervical scores ≤4.

A single 3 mg PGE_2 vaginal tablet is therefore not as effective as 450 μg of PGE_2 administered by the extra-amniotic route for ripening the cervix and inducing labour when the cervical score is low. The use of repeated vaginal tablets does have certain attractions. It is simple and produces little undesirable uterine activity after the first insertion. However, with our protocol almost a third of patients were still not in labour 24 h after the onset of treatment. The mother and foetus are unlikely to come to harm from this delay as the procedure is not invasive, but it is often upsetting to the mother and her attendants. Repeated insertion of vaginal pessaries followed by periods attached to a foetal monitor can be rather disheartening. It is possible that the problems of the vaginal tablet lie mainly in the nature of the base material and its pattern of prostaglandin release, a topic dealt with by Dr Sellers (this Symposium). An alternative is the use of a different vaginal gel. Studies have commenced to establish whether a stable gel preparations, described by Cameron (this Symposium) for induction in patients with a favourable cervix can also be used for treating the unripe cervix, and ultimately inducing labour in this group of patients. If unwanted uterine activity is to be prevented, but undue delay in the initiation of labour is to be avoided, then the dosage of PGE_2 used in any new preparation is critical.

Study II

A multi-centred dose-finding study has recently been completed. The design was double-blind and randomized. All patients had cervical scores $\leqslant 5$. At the onset of treatment $2 \cdot 5$ ml of triacetin gel containing either 1, 2 or 3 mg of PGE_2 was inserted into the posterior vaginal fornix (Table 1). If labour did not become established then a further treatment with the same dosage was given 6 h later. The indications for induction, in relation to dosage regime, are given in Table 2.

Table 1

PGE_2 triacetin gel dose finding study. Low cervical score.
Study population

| | PGE_2 dosage (mg) | | |
	1·0	2·0	3·0
Number of patients	26	24	29
Mean gestational age (weeks)	40·6	40·5	40·8
Mean maternal age (years)	24·2	26·1	27·6
Mean parity	0·6	0·5	0·7
Mean cervical score	3·9	3·6	4·2

Table 2

PGE_2 triacetin gel dose finding study. Low cervical score.
Indications for induction

| | PGE_2 dosage (mg) | | |
	1·0	2·0	3·0
Past estimated date of delivery	11	12	17
Hypertension	11	7	9
Intrauterine growth retardation	3	2	1
Poor weight profile	0	0	2
Intrauterine foetal death	0	2	0
Other	1	1	0

Table 3

PGE_2 triacetin gel dose finding study. Low cervical score.
Results

| | PGE_2 dosage (mg) | | |
	1·0	2·0	3·0
Success rate	11/25	15/24	21/27
	(44)[a]	(63)	(78)
Mean induction–delivery interval (h)	10·7	13·8	10·4
Doses of PGE_2			
1	3	6	13
2	8	9	8

[a] Figures in parentheses indicate percentages

The results are summarized in Table 3. The rate of successful induction of labour is apparently dose-related, with 78 per cent of the patients receiving 2×3 mg doses of PGE_2 being successfully induced. Once labour was established the induction-delivery interval appears to be similar, no matter which dosage was used. It is apparent that the higher dosage gave a much greater chance of inducing successful labour with a single application. These figures strongly suggest that with this new preparation, a dose of 3 mg of PGE_2 is necessary to achieve cervical ripening and induction when the cervical score is low. The fact that 22 out of the 76 patients went into labour after a single dose of PGE_2 may be considered encouraging, but it must be remembered that these patients were of mixed parity and included some with a cervical score of 5, which may not be regarded by some clinicians as particularly unfavourable. The overall success rate in the 3 mg group of 78 per cent therefore appears to be no great improvement over the results obtained using the 3 mg vaginal tablet as described in Study I.

The ideal agent for ripening the cervix and inducing labour in those patients with a low cervical score still eludes the clinician. We are still unable to differentiate between those patients who will respond well and those who will respond poorly to local prostaglandin treatment. It may be that further progress in the treatment of the unripe cervix will have to await advances in our knowledge of those factors which initiate cervical ripening and parturition.

References

Calder, A. A. and Embrey, M. P. (1975). In *Management of labour* (Ed. R. W. Beard). Royal College of Obstetricians and Gynaecologists, London.

Calder, A. A., Embrey, M. P. and Tait, T. (1977). Ripening of the cervix with extraamniotic prostaglandins E_2 in viscous gel before induction of labour. *British Journal of Obstetrics and Gynaecology* **84**, 264.

Ezimokhai, M. and Nwambinle, J. N. (1980). The use of a Foley's cathether in ripening the unfavourable cervix prior to induction of labour. *British Journal of Obstetrics and Gynaecology* **87**, 281.

Gordon, A. J. and Calder, A. A. (1977). Oestradiol applied locally to ripen the unfavourable cervix. *Lancet* **2**, 1319.

Kennedy, J. H., Stewart, P., Barlow, D. H., Millan, E. and Calder, A. A. (1982). Induction of labour: a comparison of a single prostaglandin E_2 vaginal tablet with amniotomy and intravenous oxytocin. *British Journal of Obstetrics and Gynaecology* **89**, 704.

Lackritz, N. H., Gibson, M. and Frigoletto, F. D. (1979). Pre-induction use of laminaria for the unripe cervix. *American Journal of Obstetrics and Gynecology* **136**, 340.

MacKenzie, I. Z. and Embrey, M. P. (1977). Cervical ripening with intra-vaginal prostaglandin E_2 gel. *British Medical Journal* **2**, 1381.

MacLennan, A. H., Green, R. C., Bryant-Greenwood, G. D., Greenwood, F. C. and Seamark, R. F. (1980). Ripening of the human cervix and induction of labour with purified procine relaxin. *Lancet* **1**, 220.

Mitchell, M. D., Flint, A. P. F., Bibby, J., Buent, J., Arnold, J. M., Anderson, A. B. M. and Turnbull, A. C. (1977). Rapid increases in plasma prostaglandin concentrations after vaginal examination and amniotomy. *British Medical Journal* **2**, 1183.

Mochizulki, M. and Tojo, S. (1980). Effect of dehydroepiandrosterone sulfate on softening and dilatation of the uterine cervix in pregnant women. In *Dilatation of the uterine cervix* (Eds F. Naftolin and P. G. Stubblefield). Raven Press, New York. p. 267.

Nicolaides, K. H., Welch, C. C., Koullapis, E. N. and Filshie, G. M. (1983). Cervical dilatation
        by Lamicel. *British Journal of Obstetrics and Gynaecology* **90**, 1060.
Stewart, P. (1977). Patients' attitudes to induction and labour. *British Medical Journal* **2**, 749.
Stewart, P. and Calder, A. A. (1981). Management of the unripe cervix (Letter). *British Journal
        of Obstetrics and Gynaecology* **88**, 1071.
Stewart, P., Kennedy, J. M., Barlow, D. H. and Calder, A. A. (1981). A comparison of
        oestradiol and prostaglandin E_2 for ripening the cervix. *British Journal of
        Obstetrics and Gynaecology* **88**, 236.
Stewart, P., Kennedy, J. M., Hillan, E. and Calder, A. A. (1983). The unripe cervix:
        management with vaginal or extra-amniotic prostaglandin E_2. *Journal of
        Obstetrics and Gynecology* **4**, 90.
Tromans, P. M., Beasley, J. M. and Shenouda, P. I. (1981). Comparative study of oestradiol
        and prostaglandin E_2 vaginal gel for ripening the unfavourable cervix
        before induction of labour. *British Medical Journal* **282**, 679.

Discussion

Dr Taylor wondered what general recommendations could be given for patients showing contractions but no dilatation following the first prostaglandin insertion.

Dr Stewart said that he would be cautious in giving a second dose of PGE_2 to a woman with contractions but no dilatation, because of the potential problem of hyperstimulation. He would probably give half a 3 mg tablet as the second dose.

Dr Murray commented on Dr Husslein's oxytocin stimulation test which indicated the suitability of a patient to respond to an ARM oxytocin induction. He wondered whether a prostaglandin stimulation test might give some indication of which patient would show a uterine response within, say, 45 min of administration.

Dr Stewart said that there was no way of predicting from cervical assessment which patients would labour following priming treatment with PGE_2. They knew that 50 per cent of them would do so, but individual predictions were not possible from examination of the cervix. He could not predict the value of a possible prostaglandin challenge test.

Dr Calder said that it was important not to equate success in these circumstances with uterine contractility. If the cervix were unripe, the object should be to ripen it while minimizing contractility.

Dr Ledger said that the Bishop score was not a good measure of whether the cervix would dilate under the influence of prostaglandin. Some mechanical method was required for assessing changes in the collagenous tissue of the cervix, and until such a technique were devised it would not be possible to use a prostaglandin challenge test.

Dr MacKenzie agreed that an ideal ripening agent would not stimulate myometrial activity excessively, but it seemed that effects exerted by prostaglandins beyond those exerted on the cervix itself, were also required for a successful outcome.

Dr Stewart suggested that perhaps one might ripen the cervix with oestradiol and then induce labour with prostaglandins.

Dr Read thought it important, particularly for clinicians in district general hospitals, to distinguish between ripening of the cervix and induction of labour. Currently, the two were much confused.

He favoured some modification of the oxytocin test. If a good response to prostaglandins could be obtained from those patients expected to go into labour but no response from those in whom the cervix needed ripening, then it might be possible to tailor the treatment accordingly.

Dr Calder agreed. Whilst it was also true that the Bishop score was an inadequate measure of cervical ripening, there was no doubt that when the cervix ripened and the Bishop score improved the outcome was generally good. Patients who did badly were those who, after a variety of interventions, still had low Bishop scores, together with uterine contractility which put the foetus into jeopardy. In evaluating the studies currently being presented with Bishop scores $\leqslant 5$, it was important to remember the very great difference that existed between patients with scores of say 3 and 0–1.

Prostaglandin release following vaginal prostaglandin treatment for labour induction

SUSAN SELLERS and I. Z. MACKENZIE

*Nuffield Department of Obstetrics and Gynaecology,
John Radcliffe Hospital, Headington, Oxford, UK*

Following the initial observations in 1976 in Oxford of the success of giving vaginal prostaglandins (PGs) for cervical ripening and labour induction, we noted that while the majority of patients gained considerable benefit from such treatment there were a few in whom either a ripening effect could not be produced or labour remained difficult to establish. In these latter cases there was often no evidence of any myometrial stimulation being provoked. The reverse was also occasionally noted, some women responding abruptly to the prostaglandin treatment with occasional rapid and worrying contractions and almost precipitate delivery. Attempts to measure the release of PGE_2 from vaginally administered PGs was therefore of considerable importance.

Studying the kinetics of exogenous prostaglandin E_2 given for a cervical ripening and labour induction was initially only possible by measuring plasma levels of the natural prostaglandin E_2 (PGE_2) and $F_{2\alpha}$ ($PGF_{2\alpha}$) and the primary metabolite of prostaglandin F_2, 13,14-dihydro-15-keto $PGF_{2\alpha}$ (PGFM). Concentrations of PGE_2 and $PGF_{2\alpha}$ in blood had generally not been considered worthy of study because of a very rapid metabolism, and PGFM was considered not particularly relevant when PGE_2 had been administered. During the past 2–3 years, the bicyclo-PGEM assay had been developed (Demers *et al.* 1983), measuring all PGE_2 products and thus considered to be a stable PGEM. This has therefore allowed a more direct analysis of administered PGE_2 kinetics.

Study 1. Amniotic fluid, PGE and PGF profiles following vaginal PGE₂ gel instillation

The first study we carried out in the late 1970s was to observe the change in PGE and PGF concentrations in amniotic fluid after 5 mg of PGE_2 in viscous cellulose

The role of prostaglandins in labour, edited by Clive Wood, 1985: Royal Society of Medicine Services International Congress and Symposium Series No. 92, published by Royal Society of Medicine Services Limited.

S. Sellers and I. Z. Mackenzie

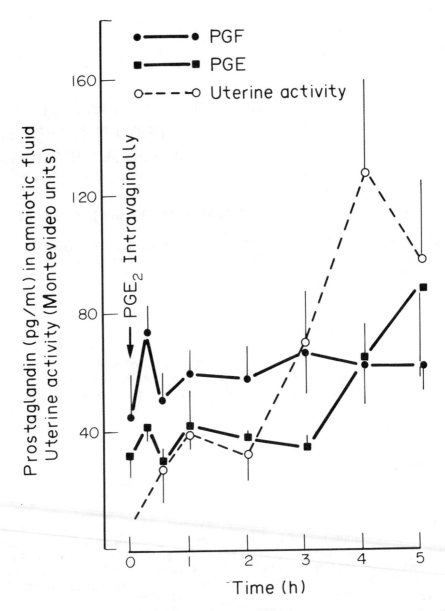

Figure 1. PGE (■ —— ■) and PGF (● —— ●) concentrations in amniotic fluid following the intravaginal administrations of 5 mg of PGE₂ viscous gel. Uterine activity (○ —— ○) is illustrated as Montevideo units.

gel had been administered intra-vaginally. Five patients, scheduled for mid-trimester abortion were studied and serial samples of amniotic fluid were collected via a transabdominal intra-amniotic catheter to be used later for administering the therapeutic abortifacient dose of PGE₂. Fig. 1 illustrates the results obtained. PGE concentrations showed a rise 2–3 h after administration of PGE₂, while there was no significant trend in PGF values. Myometrial activity, recorded using the intra-amniotic catheter and displayed as Montevideo units, increased in a similar manner to the PGE profile except it was displaced so that uterine activity occurred about 1 h after the increase in PGE levels were noted.

It had been our view in Oxford, and that of others such as Liggins (1979), that the goal for PG administration for both cervical ripening and labour induction is a sustained exposure of PGs to the cervix and uterus to produce the desired effect upon cervical state and gradually to stimulate myometrial contractions. The results, showing a rise in PGE in amniotic fluid, encouraged us to believe we were achieving this goal. However, Gordon-Wright and Elder (1979), measuring a different PGEM in peripheral maternal blood following vaginal administration of a similar PGE_2 gel preparation, showed a very rapid rise within 30 min of treatment. This led us to reconsider our findings. Earlier *in vitro* studies of PGE_2 released from viscous gel in a water bath demonstrated that about 50 per cent was released with 60 min, and this tended to support Gordon-Wright and Elder's observations (MacKenzie *et al.* 1980). The search for a slow release preparation therefore continued. Embrey succeeded in developing such a vehicle, a non-biodegradable polyethylene polymer pessary which can be manipulated to produce release profiles according to any particular requirement (Embrey *et al.* 1981). Fig. 2 compares an example of an Embrey pessary with a release half-life of 4 h with a viscous gel, and illustrates the *in vitro* release using a water bath. About 8 per cent of the incorporated PGE_2 is released per hour from the polyethylene polymer.

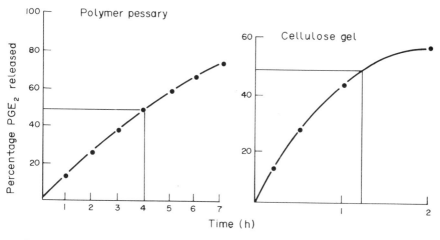

Figure 2. In vitro *release of PGE_2 from a polymer pessary with a 4 h half-life (Embrey* et al. *1980) and 5 per cent viscous cellulose gel (MacKenzie* et al. *1980).*

Study 2. *In vivo* release profiles of PGE_2 from vaginal vehicles using the bicyclo-PGEM assay

It is obviously important to look at the performance of different vehicles in clinical settings and this we have done recently using the newly-developed PGEM assay (Demers *et al.* 1983). Thirty five patients scheduled for mid-trimester abortion have been studied in groups of five. PGEM concentrations have been measured in the peripheral circulation following the vaginal instillation of 10 mg of PGE_2 administered in one of six different carrier vehicles. The vehicles investigated are those that have been used clinically: viscous cellulose gel, wax-based pessaries, oral tablets,

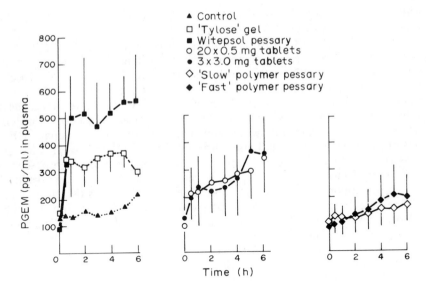

Figure 3. PGEM concentrations using the bicyclo-PGEM assay in the circulation following the vaginal instillation of 9 or 10 mg of PGE$_2$ in different carrier vehicles (from Castle et al. 1983).

vaginal tablets (9 mg of PGE$_2$) and two different polymer pessaries, one with a half-life of 4 h and the other with a half-life of 7 h.

Serial venous blood samples were collected for 6 h starting before prostaglandin treatment in all patients, including 5 patients in a control group who had not been treated with PGE$_2$. The release profiles obtained for each of the groups are shown in Fig. 3. The quickest release was from the wax-based pessaries, after which the gel provided the next quickest release, the other vehicles in general being much slower. It is clear that with all preparations there is a wide variation in 'response', as illustrated by the range of mean values and by the large standard deviation for each sampling time.

Study 3. Relationship between exogenous vaginal PGE$_2$, PGEM and labour outcome

In our final study, which has barely been completed, we have examined the release/absorption of 3 mg of PGE$_2$ from either a commercially available vaginal tablet or a wax-based Witepsol pessary. The aim of the study was to compare the two preparations by observing plasma concentrations of PGEM using the bicyclo-PGEM assay. PGFM concentrations were also determined before treatment and 3 h after treatment to investigate the possible relationships between the values obtained and cervical condition, onset of labour, labour outcome and the concentration of PGEM in the neonatal circulation at delivery.

Twenty primigravidae with an unfavourable cervix, each with a singleton pregnancy and cephalic presentation, were randomly allocated to treatment with 3 mg of PGE$_2$ as a vaginal tablet or Witepsol pessary. In all cases a peripheral blood sample was collected prior to a vaginal examination, which was performed to confirm that the modified Bishop's score was $\leqslant 4$. Treatment allocation was blinded to the clinician

(SS) during the study. Further blood samples were collected 3 h after treatment. The following morning, 15–24 h after treatment, the cervix was reassessed and formal labour induction performed if labour had not already commenced. Blood was also taken from the umbilical vessels immediately after delivery but before placental separation. All samples were assayed for PGEM and the maternal samples also assayed for PGFM. One patient in the pessary group was delivered by caesarean section 30 min after treatment because the foetal heart pattern suggested foetal distress. She has therefore been excluded from further analyses.

One of the few differences observed between the two preparations was the change in PGEM value 3 h after prostaglandin instillation (Fig. 4). Although there was no significant difference between the two groups before treatment (229 ± 128 pg/ml with the tablets; 295 ± 173 pg/ml with the pessary), at 3 h the pessary group had a significantly higher PGEM level (640 ± 430 pg/ml) compared to the tablet group (277 ± 172 pg/ml). All the former patients showed a rise in PGEM at 3 h, while 3 of the 10 patients given a tablet had lower levels at 3 h than the pre-treatment value. The mean post-3 h treatment value in the pessary group was significantly higher than the pre-treatment value ($p < 0.0001$).

In contrast, PGFM showed no significant trend in either group (Fig. 4). At induction the following morning, the cervical scores had improved in both groups, the tablet group from 3.30 ± 0.82 to 7.80 ± 3.33 ($p < 0.0001$) and the pessary group from 3.67 ± 0.71 to 8.44 ± 3.84 ($p < 0.0001$). More women went into labour following

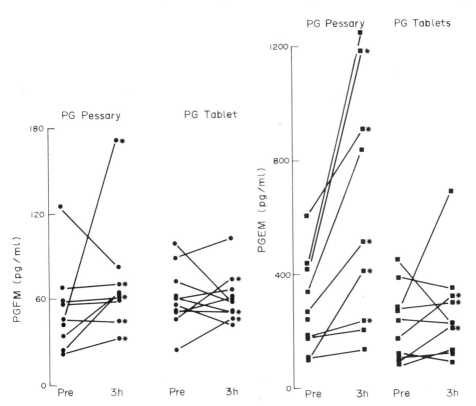

Figure 4. PGEM and PGFM concentrations in venous plasma before and 3 h after the vaginal administration of 3 mg of PGE₂ in a Witepsol pessary or dry tablet to ripen the cervix. The asterisks indicate the patients who proceeded to established labour.

treatment with the pessary (5 of 9) compared with the tablets (3 of 10). The treatment to delivery intervals were shorter in the pessary group ($20 \cdot 33 \pm 8 \cdot 61$ h); the length of labour was also shorter in the pessary group ($7 \cdot 44 \pm 4 \cdot 92$ h) compared with the tablet group ($8 \cdot 55 \pm 5 \cdot 21$ h) and the mean maximum oxytocin requirement was less following pessary treatment ($13 \cdot 33 \pm 21 \cdot 33$ mU/min) than with the tablets ($20 \cdot 80 \pm 23 \cdot 40$ mU/min). None of these differences reached statistical significance.

Considering all patients together there appeared to be remarkably little association between pre-existing PGEM and PGFM values and cervical condition, the ease with which labour could be induced or the subsequent length of the first stage of labour. Nor were any significant relationships found between the PGEM and PGFM values recorded 3 h after treatment and any of these indices. The only significant positive correlation was between the change in PGEM level at 3 h compared to the pre-treatment value and the duration of the first stage of labour ($r = 0 \cdot 497$, $p = 0 \cdot 0302$; Fig. 5). However, PGFM changes and duration of the first stage did not correlate significantly.

The striking correlation between the concentration of PGEM in the umbilical vessels at delivery and the interval between maternal treatment with prostaglandin and delivery supports the view that PGEM levels in the peripheral circulation are probably an accurate reflection of the absorption of exogenous prostaglandin from the vagina.

The neonates delivered soon after PGE_2 treatment had higher PGEM levels in both umbilical artery and vein compared with those delivered after many hours ($p = 0 \cdot 0048$ vein, $p = 0 \cdot 0002$ artery; Fig. 6). However, there was no correlation with pre-treatment or 3 h post-treatment maternal PGEM values. PGFM was not measured

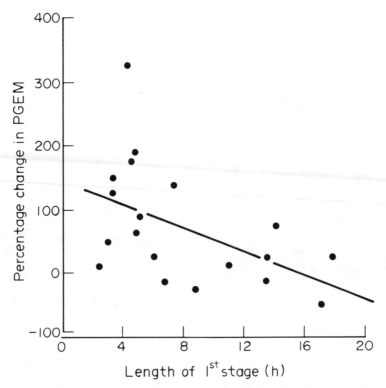

Figure 5. Percentage change in PGEM concentrations in maternal venous plasma 3 h after vaginal PGE₂ treatment in relation to the length of the first stage of labour in 19 patients.

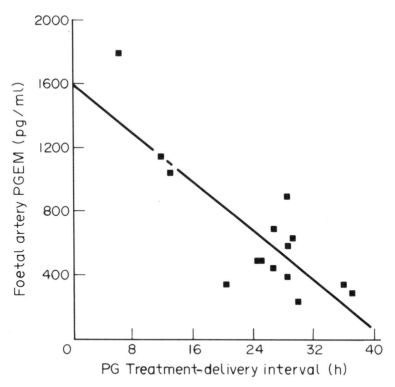

Figure 6. Relationship between the interval from PGE$_2$ treatment to delivery and the concentration of PGEM in the umbilical artery at delivery in 15 patients.

in the cord samples. We have previously shown (MacKenzie *et al.* 1980) that the neonates born to mothers whose labours were induced with PGE$_2$ have higher PGE in cord venous plasma at delivery than is found in those born following conventional induction, spontaneous labour or elective caesarean section. PGF levels were found to be similar in all the labouring groups.

As mentioned, these latter results are as yet not completely analysed but they do not immediately show any startling correlations between labour patterns or outcome and PGEM or PGFM concentrations at the time examined. However, much more work needs to be done in this area before definite conclusions can be reached.

Acknowledgements

We acknowledge the following who collaborated in the collection of these data: Dr Bruce Castle who helped in clinical management, Sister Jane Ferguson for expert nursing care, and Joan Bellinger for performing the prostaglandin assays.

References

Castle, B. M., Bellinger, J., Brennecke, S., Embrey, M. P. and MacKenzie, I. Z. (1983). *In vivo* studies using the bicyclo PGEM assay to assess release of PGE$_2$ from vaginal preparations used for labour induction. Abstracts of the British Congress on Obstetrics and Gynaecology, Birmingham, July 1983.

Demars, L. M., Brennecke, S. P., Mountford, L. A., Brunt, J. D. and Turnbull, A. C. (1983). Development and validation of a radioimmunoassay for prostaglandin E_2 metabolite levels in plasma. *Journal of Clinical Endocrinology and Metabolism* **57**, 101.

Embrey, M. P., Graham, N. B. and McNeill, M. E. (1980). Induction of labour with a sustained-release prostaglandin E_2 vaginal pessary. *British Medical Journal* **28**, 901.

Gordon-Wright, A. P. and Elder, M. G. (1979). The systemic absorption from the vagina of prostaglandin E_2 administered for the induction of labour. *Prostaglandins* **18**, 153.

Liggins, G. C. (1979). Controlled trial of induction of labour by vaginal suppositories containing prostaglandin E_2. *Prostaglandins* **18**, 167.

MacKenzie, I. Z., Bradley, S. and Mitchell, M. D. (1980). Prostaglandin levels in cord venous plasma at delivery related to labour. In *Advances in prostaglandin and thromboxane research* (Eds B. Samuelsson, P. W. Ramswell and R. Paoletti). Vol. 8. Raven Press, New York. p. 1401.

MacKenzie, I. Z., Burnett, F. R. and Embrey, M. P. (1980). *In vitro* studies of the release of prostaglandins from viscous solutions. *British Journal of Obstetrics and Gynaecology* **87**, 292.

MacKenzie, I. Z. and Mitchell, M. D. (1981). Serial determinations of PGE_2 levels in amniotic fluid following vaginal administration of a PGE_2 gel. *Prostaglandins and Medicine* **7**, 43.

Discussion

Dr Gordon-Wright asked the Oxford group about the origin of the PGE_2 in the foetal circulation. He wondered whether this was the PGE_2 that had been administered.

Dr MacKenzie thought that it was. However, it was not apparently related to the systemic level. There was little correlation between PGEM in the maternal circulation at an earlier stage of labour and the level found in the umbilical cord vessels at delivery.

Dr Calder said in his experience using the vaginal tablet, little uterine contractility was found during the first 3 h.

Dr MacKenzie said that they had not so far compared the tocograph for the tablet and the pessary.

Dr Ledger said that in a study in the sheep which they had performed with Dr Dennis Bowsher from Auckland, they found a plexus of veins and arteries running from the vagina to the uterus over the serosal surface of the cervix. It seemed likely that blood flowed in both directions in this plexus, and it was possible, in the sheep at least, that prostaglandins placed in the vagina by-passed the cervix entirely and moved directly into the systemic circulation.

Dr Calder said that a clinical impression had been recorded by some workers that a vaginal tablet put into the anterior vaginal fornix was more effective than one inserted posteriorly. This might reflect a difference in blood supply.

Dr MacKenzie said that they had measured PGE_2 in amniotic fluid and PGEM in the peripheral circulation. Nonetheless, there did appear to be a substantial delay between the increase in prostaglandin concentration in amniotic fluid and that in the blood. In the presence of a vascular plexus however, one might expect the PGE levels to rise in the amniotic fluid more quickly.

Dr Ledger said that, on the contrary, the presence of such a plexus would ensure the take-up of prostaglandin and its delivery to the periphery before its entry into the amniotic fluid, as Dr MacKenzie's results suggested.

Dr Keirse said that one would clearly expect a delay in entering into the amniotic fluid because, in order to get there, it had to pass through the circulation and then through the foetus. He was aware that suggestions had been made that prostaglandins deposited in the vagina passed through the cervical os, but he did not think that they were correct.

Dr Gordon-Wright said that in his own studies he showed slower systemic absorption from the tablet than the gel. However, the clinical outcome was similar for patients treated by both procedures and he wondered whether the time course of absorption was important.

Dr MacKenzie thought that a slower rate of absorption might actually be advantageous if uterine activity were stimulated, but at an initially low rate.

Dr Husslein said that his own group had measured PGEM levels before during and after infusion of PGE_2. The correlation which they obtained between the amount infused and the amount detected gave them confidence in the assay. Unfortunately, they had terminated their observations 3 h after infusion since they had expected no further effects. They had concluded that local application, sufficient to ripen the cervix at term, did not load the circulation to the same extent as prostaglandins used intravenously. This conclusion also correlated with the fact that they saw no systemic side-effects after local application. In contrast to the findings of some other workers, they did not find major absorption after endocervical instillation, although the low doses that they were employing ($0 \cdot 4 - 0 \cdot 5$ mg) might account for this difference.

Even so, individual absorption was very variable. At one stage they had devised a delivery system to apply aqueous prostaglandin locally to the cervix. In one patient such an application produced massive uterine hyperstimulation and rapid increase in PGEM levels but both came back to normal values following removal of the application. He felt that this individual variability might be responsible for some patients going into labour very rapidly and for the foetal problems that might result from hyperstimulation.

Dr MacKenzie said that in Oxford Dr Brenneke had infused himself with PGE_2 and obtained a good correlation between infusion rate and circulating PGEM levels. He wondered what systemic levels were necessary to induce gastrointestinal side-effects.

Dr Husslein said that effects were seen at 1000–2000 pg/ml of PGEM.

Dr Gordon-Wright had patients who vomited with intravaginal preparations. One had responded after receiving 5 mg in a wax base with serum levels in the order of 2000 pg/ml. Another was a patient inadvertently given two 3 mg PGE_2 tablets at once.

Dr Calder wondered whether uterine contractility was usually well established before a circulating rise in prostaglandins was demonstrated.

Dr Gordon-Wright said that such a pattern certainly did occur in some patients. Conversely, one might find marked rises in systemic absorption without any apparent effect on the uterus.

Prostaglandin induction in women with low Bishop scores

S. M. WALTON

Department of Obstetrics and Gynaecology,
North Tees General Hospital, Stockton-on-Tees, Cleveland, UK

We have examined the efficacy of vaginal prostaglandin gel in inducing patients with low Bishop scores. During the trial a total of 17 patients were studied. The admission criteria and treatment schedules are outlined in Table 1. A starting dose of 1 mg of prostaglandin (PG) E_2 was given intravaginally. If, after 6 h, the patient was not having regular contractions and the cervix had not dilated to at least 2 cm, then a second dose of 2 mg of PGE_2 in gel was given. If contractions were present during that time, 1 mg of PGE_2 in gel was administered. The efficacy of the regime was assessed at 12 h, and only those patients who were in established labour with regular contractions and who had shown cervical dilatation of at least 2 cm were considered to be successes.

The results are shown in Table 2. Seven patients were considered failures as determined by the protocol. The figures are too small to extrapolate any trends but it is clear that, as expected, multiparous patients responded better than primiparous ones. Of the failures, only 2 did not respond to repeated prostaglandin and eventual

Table 1

Prostaglandin gel study. Admission criteria and
treatment schedule

Admission criteria:	18–35 years old
	$\geqslant 36$ weeks of pregnancy
	Singleton pregnancy
	Intact membranes
	Bishop score < 4
Treatment schedule:	
Induction:	PGE_2 1 mg in gel
At 6 h:	PGE_2 1 or 2 mg
At 12 h:	Assessment — success
	partial success
	failure

The role of prostaglandins in labour, edited by Clive Wood, 1985: Royal Society of Medicine Services International Congress and Symposium Series No. 92, published by Royal Society of Medicine Services Limited.

Table 2

Prostaglandin gel study. Results

	Bishop score	Number	Failures
Primigravidae ($n = 11$)	4	5	—
	3	4	3
	2	2	2
Multigravidae ($n = 6$)	4	2	—
	3	3	1
	2	0	—
	1	1	1

surgical induction, requiring caesarean section for delivery. The remainder successfully went into labour by a more formal form of induction (Table 3).

From the beginning of the trial we had reservations about the protocol, particularly the definition of success and failure, as it was felt that the criteria adopted were not appropriate for this form of induction. The times for which the patients were in established labour (7·4–10·6 h) were within clinically accepted limits but obviously outside the 12 h study period as determined by the induction–delivery intervals (16·9–26·6 h). Of possible relevance may be the fact that vaginal prostaglandin is used in a different manner to the traditional methods of induction.

Table 3

Prostaglandin gel study. Modes of delivery

Delivery:	Spontaneous	6
	Instrumental	4
	Caesarean section	6
Indications for caesarean section:		
	Foetal distress	3
	Failure to progress	1
	Failed induction	2

Table 4 shows our present schedule at North Tees Hospital for inducing labour in patients who have 'middle risk' indications, e.g. post-dates, mild hypertension, suspected growth problems. The emphasis is on maintaining a fairly 'low profile', keeping patients in the familiar surroundings of the ante-natal ward, fully ambulant until they are in established labour when monitoring is required.

Table 4

North Tees Hospital induction schedule for patients at 'middle risk'

Decision and CTG
Light breakfast
Prostin E_2 3 mg vaginal tablet
Ambulation
VE prior to meals
CTG when contracting
(Prostin E_2 3 mg repeated at 24 and 48 h)
Transfer to labour ward in established labour

Table 5
North Tees Hospital clinical results with Prostin E₂. Dosage requirements

Dose (mg)	Post dates	Hypertension	Intrauterine growth retardataion	Miscellaneous
3	36	29	14	13
6	4	10	1	2
9	3	4	3	1
12	—	3	—	—

During a 6 month period, 123 of our patients have had this form of induction. Table 5 shows that 74·8 per cent of patients required only a single dose of the 3 mg PGE_2 vaginal prostaglandin tablet. The fact that only 16·3 per cent of our post-dates patients compared with 37 per cent of hypertensives required more than a single dose is probably more a reflection of gestation than other factors. The cervical scores showed no demonstrable differences between the 2 groups. Most patients had cervical dilatation of less than 2 cm at the onset of induction.

Induction–delivery intervals for the 3 mg responders ranged from 12–15 h after 'induction'. The recorded length of labour (3·3–8·8 h) showed acceptable short labours even in patients requiring more than a single dose of prostaglandin. More important however, was the fact that 69 per cent of our patients spent less than 6 h in the labour ward (Table 6). Delivery in these patients, with a caesarean section rate of 9·8 per cent, compares well with the over-all hospital rate of 13 per cent. Although there were no caesarean sections for failed induction, 7 failures on the regime were identified and these required more formal induction or went into spontaneous labour. Two patients had complications from the regime. One patient developed type II dips 4 h after insertion of the pessary requiring emergency caesarean section, and another had a stellate tear in the vagina possibly due to a precipitate labour.

Table 6
North Tees Hospital clinical results with Prostin E₂. Time spent in labour ward (h)

	<3	6	12	18	Unclassified
Post dates	20	9	8	3	2
Hypertension	20	12	9	1	—
Intrauterine growth retardation	9	5	2	—	2
Miscellaneous	5	5	3	1	—

Table 7
North Tees Hospital clinical experience with Prostin E₂. Advantages of regime

Fully ambulant patient
'Low tech' surroundings
Reduces time in labour ward
Reduces immobilization time
Simulates 'natural' onset of labour
No change in maternal or perinatal morbidity
Indicates alternative clinical and research potentials
of PG gel

Our clinical experience was that vaginal prostaglandin given in this way was acceptable to the staff and more particularly to the patients (Table 7). They remained ambulant in familiar 'low tech' surroundings and experienced a more 'natural onset of labour' at a time when consumer pressure demands 'normal childbirth'. We feel that this clinical experience has high-lighted the fact that, with vaginal prostaglandins, different criteria and time schedules are necessary fully to evaluate the potential of this form of induction.

Discussion

Dr Murray wondered whether, since most responders declared themselves after the first or second dose, there was justification for setting an arbitrary limit to the total number of doses that would be tried before alternative means of induction.

Dr Walton said that analysis of their own experience had certainly led them to change their standard clinical protocol. It might be more appropriate to give only 2 doses, but give the second dose earlier, and then go on to more formal methods of induction.

Dr MacKenzie said that his group had analysed retrospectively their treatment of unfavourable primiparous patients. Those that had been treated in the evening but whose cervices were not ripe the following morning had been arbitrarily given either vaginal treatment or intravenous oxytocin with amniotomy where possible. There was little difference in the results between the 2 groups. The duration of labour was similar and the ultimate caesarean section rate was also similar, though relatively high in these non-responders. If one treatment failed to work he was not convinced that anything was gained by administering the second one.

Dr Walton said that one of the deciding factors in adopting their later protocol was the fact that patients did not like the 'high tech' surroundings of the labour ward. They preferred to be ambulant in the ante-natal ward with some form of monitoring.

Dr Murray said that limiting treatment to 2 doses had another aspect. Examining Dr Stewart's data from 13 primigravid patients with unripe cervices one might say that although 86·7 per cent had responded by the second dose, of the 8 remaining, half responded to the third dose. And it was in this latter group, of whom only 50 per cent would respond, that an alternative had to be found.

Dr Walton agreed. Two doses accounted for 90 per cent of responses. One was then left with 10 per cent of non-responding patients who required more formal methods of induction.

Dr MacKenzie wondered what had been the experience of the other Panellists using the Upjohn triacetin gel for either the ripe or unripe cervix.

Dr Read had used it for patients with high Bishop scores and had 87 evaluable cases. He endorsed Dr Stewart's comments on patient acceptability. Many patients were much happier with the 'low tech' approach. Of his 87 cases, 39 were multigravid women who had the gel and of these 39, 19 had previously had a labour induced by oxytocin and amniotomy. Of these 19, 17 agreed that they were happier with the gel induction. He also had the impression of a lower requirement for analgesia, perhaps because the patients were ambulant and could adopt a more comfortable position or could simply distract themselves more readily.

Dr MacKenzie agreed that those administering vaginal prostaglandins had the impression that it was much more acceptable. However, he cautioned against comparing the memory of a first labour, induced by oxytocin, with that of a second induced by PGs. First labours were generally more unpleasant, and one could need to perform a randomized trial properly to assess the patients' views.

Dr Lee agreed that women receiving the prostaglandin gel had a high success rate. Following delivery he had asked them how they felt about it and his conclusions were similar to those of Dr Read. Patients were quite comfortable during labour. They could walk around and his impression was that they required less analgesia.

Dr Hinchley said that analgesia requirements had been recorded and so could subsequently be analysed. However, she said that the low Bishop score study had been abandoned because of a high failure rate in primiparous patients and they needed to revise the dose before the trial was re-started. It seemed that either a higher starting dose or a shorter dosing interval was required, and she wondered which Panellists felt was more appropriate.

Dr Walton said that it was difficult to see any trend as to which patients would respond and which would require higher doses. Since there seemed to be no consistency, he thought it essential to start with the 1 mg dose. Though there were reasons for going straight to the 2 mg he had patients delivering within 1·5 h of the 1 mg dose, an effect which they could not have predicted.

Dr MacKenzie wondered why, since there was a 3 mg tablet, no 3 mg gel existed.

Dr Hinchley said that in Dr Stewart's dose-finding study some patients who received 2 mg or 3 mg initial doses had very precipitate labours. For reasons of safety it was therefore decided that all patients should have a 1 mg initial dose, which was found to cause rapid labour in only a few individuals.

Dr Stewart said that there were no precipitate labours in patients with low Bishop scores even on the 3 mg preparation. The rapid labours had occurred in multigravid patients with favourable cervices who received 3 mg in the dose-finding study. After 2 or 3 had delivered fairly rapidly the 1 mg was introduced. However, if one wished to assess the effect of the new gel on the unripe cervix it was a mistake to have patients of mixed parity. For nulliparous parents with genuinely low score ($\leqslant 4$) he thought that 3 mg was an appropriate starting dose. If one were to extend the entry criteria then he agreed it was necessary to bring the starting dose down.

Dr Cameron suggested that the timing of the assessment should be reduced from 6 to 4 h.

Dr Calder said that using the 3 mg vaginal tablet they had been reluctant to shorten the dosing interval to <6 h. However, if absorption from the gel was rapid and if no effect was observed by 4 h, it seemed reasonable to repeat the dose at that time.

Dr MacKenzie suggested that the timing of the second dose was also a matter of logistics. One did not want to establish labour at 7.00 p.m. and the timing of treatment, particularly for women with an unfavourable cervix, required some thought.

Dr Murray said that his earlier remarks referred to patients with an unfavourable cervix. Whilst it was true that patient acceptability was high, the duration of the procedure had to be explained to the patient, who would otherwise be dissatisfied in not seeing the instant results that they would expect from an amniotomy. He felt that 4 h between administrations was a reasonable interval, because they were used to 4 h examinations on the labour wards, and because the procedure would be slightly accelerated for the patient. However, it was necessary to have a 1 mg test dose in the first instance so as not to achieve an over-response.

Dr MacKenzie therefore suggested that the consensus view for the ripe cervix was an initial administration of 1 mg with re-examination at 4 h and a repeat of the dose if necessary. For the unripe cervix the procedure was a 3 mg initial dose, again with reassessment after 4 h and a repeat administration if necessary.

Dr Calder agreed. He repeated the fact that Dr Walton's data had shown clear differences between individuals assessed with a Bishop score of 4 or more and those whose scores were lower. It was really a waste of time giving a dose of 1 mg to a patient with a score $\leqslant 3$.

Dr Stewart said that in a study he had performed with Dr Kennedy and Dr Calder a 3 mg PGE$_2$ tablet was used in multigravid patients with ripe cervices. They received 1 tablet and their membranes were ruptured 4 h later. That was sufficient to put all of them into labour. This therefore seemed a reasonable protocol for the multigravid patient with a ripe cervix, although one might perhaps use 2 mg of gel as opposed to a 3 mg tablet. However, once contractions had started then the membranes could be ruptured 4 h later.

Dr MacKenzie said that if Upjohn were to restart their trial then a randomized comparison of a 3 mg PGE$_2$ gel with a 3 mg PGE$_2$ tablet would allow objective assessment of the results.

European multi-centre trial of intra-cervical PGE$_2$ in triacetin gel. Report on the Leiden data

M. J. N. C. KEIRSE, H. H. H. KANHAI, R. A. VERWEY and J. BENNEBROEK GRAVENHORST

Department of Obstetrics and Gynaecology, University of Leiden Medical Centre, Netherlands

In the presence of a ripe cervix, successful induction of labour will be readily achieved by most of the methods that are presently available. Effectiveness of induction becomes a major concern, however, when the cervix is unripe. The alternatives of opting for caesarean section or for continuation of pregnancy until the induction prospects have become either more favourable or superfluous, do not appear to be acceptable. Pre-induction cervical ripening or cervical softening then becomes appropriate (Calder 1979), although it can be debated whether such procedure should be distinct or would, on the contrary, form an integrated part of the entire induction process (MacKenzie 1981).

Prostaglandins are believed to be involved in the structural and biochemical changes that constitute cervical ripening (Ellwood and Anderson 1981) and a large number of reports have dealt with the clinical use of prostaglandins, prostaglandin E$_2$ (PGE$_2$) in particular, for pre-induction cervical ripening. Various doses and routes of administration have been tested (Calder 1979, MacKenzie 1981), but relatively few of the studies have been randomized controlled trials, that meet the requirements for incorporation in the Register of Controlled Trials in Perinatal Medicine (Grant and Chalmers 1981). Most of these have used sample sizes which are so small that real clinical benefits may have been either overlooked or exaggerated as a result of chance (Grant and Chalmers 1985). In addition, several of these trials have included patients with cervical features that would not be considered as unfavourable by most clinicians. For instance, the trials of Weiss *et al.* (1975) and Golbus and Creasy (1977) reported on patients who already had a mean Bishop score (Bishop 1964) of 5 or more before treatment began.

It is reasonable to suggest that deficiencies in the quality of the available evidence result largely from the rarity of the combination of an unripe cervix with a need for induction. But consequently, it remains difficult to assess the true clinical benefits of pre-induction cervical ripening from the scientific evidence available. Following

The role of prostaglandins in labour, edited by Clive Wood, 1985: Royal Society of Medicine Services International Congress and Symposium Series No. 92, published by Royal Society of Medicine Services Limited.

encouraging reports on the efficacy of 0·5 mg PGE_2 administered intracervically in a triacetin gel (Floberg *et al.* 1983, Thiery *et al.* 1984), we therefore participated in a multi-centre trial of this endocervical PGE_2 gel before induction of labour.

Methods

Our study at Leiden University Medical Centre was intended to assess the utility, safety and efficacy of a single, intra-cervical administration of 0·5 mg PGE_2 in 2·5 ml triacetin gel prior to induction of labour with oxytocin in patients with unfavourable cervical features and poor induction prospects. It was part of a randomized open-label multi-centre clinical trial, in which centres from 9 European and 2 African countries entered a total of more than 800 patients. Patients were randomly allocated to receive either the PGE_2 medicated gel or no drug treatment the evening (12 h) before induction of labour by intravenous oxytocin. As the study, coordinated by Dr M. Noah and Dr J. M. Decoster, ended in the second half of 1984, data on the total population studied will become available soon. This preliminary report is limited to the 50 patients (25 PGE_2 treated case and 25 control cases) studied in Leiden.

To be eligible for entry to the Leiden sector of the trial, which was approved by the local ethical committee, patients needed to be between 16 and 40 years of age, 35 weeks pregnant or more with intact membranes, but in the absence of labour. A further criterion was the presence of a live singleton foetus with a cephalic presentation. Patients were entered only if they had a medical reason for induction, had given informed consent and had a Bishop score of $\leqslant 5$ (Bishop 1964). Women with previous caesarean section or major uterine surgery, with contraindications for vaginal delivery (e.g. placenta praevia) or with a history of vaginal bleeding, threatened preterm labour or previous induction attempts in the present pregnancy were excluded, as were those or parity $\geqslant 6$. To avoid observer bias in the selection of patients, the open randomization list was replaced by a consecutively numbered sealed envelope system and then destroyed.

All patients had a full examination, including Bishop score and a 30 min cardiotocogram at entry to the study on the evening before induction. In patients allocated to the control group no further measures were undertaken for 12 h. In those allocated to PGE_2 administration, a flexible Portex catheter was inserted into the cervix under direct vision, using a speculum and full aseptic technique, until the tip touched the membranes and 2.5 ml of triacetin gel containing 0·5 mg PGE_2 was then injected from a unidose syringe. Cardiotography was continued for at least 1 h after insertion of the gel and was instituted again in both control and treated patients as soon as contractions or other events such as pain or rupture of the membranes occurred. Otherwise patients were allowed to rest for the night.

Twelve hours after insertion of the gel or allocation to the control group patients were reassessed. If not in labour, induction was started by intravenous infusion or oxytocin according to a strict schedule of doubling doses up to a maximum of 16 mU/min. Unless delivery occurred sooner, this was continued for at least 12 h before a decision was reached as to whether the procedure had been successful or not. In both groups, amniotomy was to be performed only after labour induction had been achieved with an increase in cervical dilatation of at least 3 cm. If labour had not been successfully induced after 12 h the procedure was considered a failure and subsequent management was left to the discretion of the attending obstetrician. All induction attempts and labours were monitored by cardiotocography and additional medication, vital signs and labour parameters were recorded throughout.

The characteristics of the patients studied are shown in Table 1. Both groups were comparable with the exception of maternal weight which was on average greater in the control group (82·1 kg) than in the PGE$_2$ group (74·2 kg). Gestational ages ranged from 35 to 44 weeks in both groups with a mean ±SD of 39·2±1·6 weeks in the PGE$_2$ group and 39·9±2·4 weeks in the controls. Two-thirds of the patients were nulliparous and 7 (39 per cent) of the 18 parous patients had a history of foetal death in a previous pregnancy. Several patients had more than one reason for induction. Table 1 lists the pathologies and indications for induction that occurred in more than 10 per cent of the population studied. Bishop scores at the beginning of the observation period before application of PGE$_2$ gel are also shown. All patients had a score ⩽5 and 74 per cent scored ⩽3.

Table 1

Patient details

	PGE$_2$ $(n=25)$	Control $(n=25)$	Total $(n=50)$
P/G Primigravid	13	12	25
Nulliparous	16	16	32
Parous	9	9	18
Pathology and/or reasons for induction			
Hypertensive disorders	13	15	28
Foetal growth retardation	8	4	12
Post-term (>42 weeks)	2	7	9
Pre-term (<37 weeks)	3	4	7
Diabetes	4	2	6
Albuminuria	8	5	13
Foetal death in previous pregnancy	5	2	7
Bishop score at entry in the trial			
0–1	0	2	2
2–3	19	16	35
4–5	6	7	13

Results

Table 2 summarizes the events that occurred during the 12 h observation period. No problems were encountered at the administration of the gel, though some leakage of the gel into the vagina was noted in 3 cases. For only 2 patients in the PGE$_2$ treated group was the observation period entirely uneventful as compared to an uneventful course in 24 of the 25 control patients. The most common observations in the PGE$_2$ treated group were low back pain and (painful) contraction. Not infrequently the pain sensations appeared to be disproportionately great when compared with objective measures of uterine contractility. Overall, 68 per cent of the PGE$_2$ treated patients thus required either an epidural block ($n=5$) or one or more injections of pethidine to afford adequate analgesia during the observation period.

In the control group, only 1 patient went into active labour within the 12 h observation period. She still required oxytocin later, and delivered 20 h after the

Table 2

Events occurring within the first 12 h following administration of PGE₂ gel or no drug

Events	PGE₂ (n = 25)	Control (n = 25)	P value
No events	2	24	<0·001
Contractions and/or low back pain	23	1	<0·001
Rupture of membranes	10	0	<0·005
(spontaneous + artificial)	(6 + 4)		
Active labour	15	1	<0·001
Analgesia needed	17	0	<0·001
Delivery	10	0	<0·005
(excluding caesarean sections)	8	0	<0·01

beginning of the observation period. In the PGE₂ treated group, 15 patients (60 per cent) went into active labour during the 12 h observation period and 8 of them delivered within these first 12 h. A further 2 patients in the PGE₂ group were delivered by caesarean section during the observation period because of foetal distress and late decelerations on cardiotocography. Neither of these patients was judged to be in labour at the time and the decelerations occurred in response to minimal uterine contractility. They were attributed to postmaturity (gestational age 43·5 weeks) in one case and to severe foetal growth retardation at 35·5 weeks in the other. Both infants required resuscitation and had Apgar scores of 2 at 1 min and 7 at 5 min but both had an uneventful neonatal course and follow-up at 2 months of age.

Bishop scores between entry into the study and induction of labour (12 h later) or rupture of the membranes, whichever occurred first, showed a mean (±SD) increase of 5·8 ± 3.0 points in the treatment group as compared to 0·8 ± 1·2 points in the control group ($p < 0·001$). Table 3 shows the increments in Bishop score at the end of the observation period for those patients who were still undelivered at that time, stratified by their initial Bishop score. Seven of the 15 PGE₂ treated patients who were not delivered at the end of the observation period showed an improvement in Bishop score of 5 points or more (range: 6–9) as compared to none of 25 in the control group (<0·001). In the latter group, only 2 patients had an increase of more than 2 points. As it can be argued that an improvement in Bishop score — in so far as it reflects induction prospects — is only of relevance for those patients who subsequently require formal induction of labour, it should be pointed out that only 8 patients (Table 4) in the PGE₂ group required formal induction. Of them, 3 had an increase of 3–4 points and 2 and increase of 6 points.

In the control group, the first induction attempt by oxytocin infusion for at least 12 h, up to 16 mU/min and with a total dose of more than 14 Units, failed in 72 per cent. Of these 18 women (Table 4), 11 were nulliparous and 7 parous. In the PGE₂ group only 2 first induction attempts failed. Both patients were nulliparae and both belonged to the cases (n = 3) in whom leakage of the gel into the vagina had been observed.

Consequently, only 2 (8 per cent) of the 25 patients in the PGE₂ treated group were not delivered within 24 h after entry in the study as compared to 20 patients (80 per cent) in the control group (Table 5). As shown in Tables 4 and 5, the need for oxytocin induction, the success of induction and delivery within 24 h in the PGE₂ group were not different for patients with an initial Bishop score of 2–3 than for those with scores of 4–5.

Table 3

Changes in Bishop score at the end of 12 h observation period in relation to Bishop score at admission in patients not delivered during the observation period

| Score at entry | Treatment group | No. of cases | Increase in Bishop score | | |
			0–2	3–4	5
0–1	PGE$_2$	0	0	0	0
	Control	2	2	0	0
2–3	PGE$_2$	12	1	4	7
	Control	16	14	2	0
4–5	PGE$_2$	3	2	1	0
	Control	7	7	0	0
All cases	PGE$_2$	15	3	5	7
	Control	25	23	1	0

Table 4

Success at first induction attempt in relation to Bishop score at entry

| Score at entry | Treatment group | No. of cases | First induction attempt | | |
			Not necessary	Successful	Not successful
0–1	PGE$_2$	0	0	0	0
	Control	2	0	0	2
2–3	PGE$_2$	19	13	5	1
	Control	16	1	2	13
4–5	PGE$_2$	6	4	1	1
	Control	7	0	4	3
All cases	PGE$_2$	25	17	6	2
	Control	25	1	6	18

Table 5

Interval between PGE$_2$ administration or observation and delivery in relation to initial Bishop score

| Score at entry | Treatment group | No. of cases | Hours until delivery | | |
			< 24	⩾ 24	> 48
0–1	PGE$_2$	0	0	0	0
	Control	2	0	2	2
2–3	PGE$_2$	19	18	1	1
	Control	16	3	13	8
4–5	PGE$_2$	6	5	1	1
	Control	7	2	5	2
All cases	PGE$_2$	25	23	2	2
	Control	25	5	20	12

Discussion

Table 6 gives an overview of the frequency of all outcomes which could be considered as either 'poor' or 'less desirable'. These data and those presented in Tables 2-5 clearly demonstrate the effectiveness of PGE_2 gel administration. The data further seem to confirm our suspicions that, in a sizeable proportion of patients, some of the gel entered the extra-ovular space instead of being confined exclusively to the cervical canal. This may well relate to the injection technique and can in part be attributed to the use of the soft, flexible, ungraded catheter. Thus the method not only induced cervical ripening. In the majority of patients it induced labour as well. In fact, more women had labour effectively induced by the use of the PGE_2 gel alone without oxytocin than by 12 h of oxytocin administration without PGE_2 pretreatment (60 per cent versus 28 per cent; $p < 0.05$).

While the high efficacy of the PGE_2 gel treatment thus seems to be most promising, we cannot recommend liberal adoption of the present PGE_2 pre-treatment schedule for medically indicated inductions unless clear benefits in terms of foetal and neonatal outcome can be demonstrated. Indeed, the frequent occurrence of events overnight (Table 2) and the concomitant need for adequate maternal and foetal monitoring in such cases put the ability to rest on the part of both mothers and staff at a premium. Failed induction attempts with oxytocin alone tend to have

Table 6

Incidence of poor outcome measures and side-effects

	PGE_2 ($n = 25$)	Control ($n = 25$)	P value
Effectiveness related			
Not delivered within 48 h	2	12	<0.005
Not delivered within 24 h	2	20	<0.001
Not delivered vaginally within 24 h	4	20	<0.001
Need for caesarean section	2	2	n.s.
Need for instrumental delivery			
(including caesarean section)	7	8	n.s
Need for more than one induction attempt	2	14	<0.001
Pregnant with less than 3 points increase			
in Bishop score at the end of the			
observation period	3	23	<0.001
Maternal			
Need for analgesia	23	19	n.s.
(number of epidural blocks)	(8)	(12)	
Uterine hypertonus	1	3	n.s.
Blood loss in excess of 500 ml	8	10	n.s.
Vomiting	12	6	n.s.
Foetal and neonatal			
Foetal heart rate abnormalities	8	6	n.s.
Apgar score below 7 at 1 min	8	4	n.s.
Apgar score below 7 at 5 min	1	0	n.s.
Umbilical venous pH <7.20	3	2	n.s.
No spontaneous respiration at birth	1	2	n.s.
Meconium aspiration	0	1	n.s.
Neonatal convulsions	0	1	n.s.

n.s. = not significant

a similar effect, though more on the equanimity of patients and staff than on their ability to rest. The onus may therefore well be on the choice of a more appropriate timing of the PGE$_2$ gel administration in order to accommodate both equanimity and rest.

In conclusion, it should be noted that statistical differences in outcome measures (Table 6) between the 2 groups were found only for parameters relating to the shortening of pregnancy and to the efficiency of labour. In this small series, these effects did not result in differences in caesarean section rates nor in the incidence of instrumental delivery. Similarly, there was no difference in any of the foetal or neonatal outcomes. There was perhaps a slight (non-significant) tendency toward lower Apgar score in the PGE$_2$ treated group but this was counteracted by the fact that all of the more serious outcomes, such as meconium aspiration and neonatal convulsions, occurred in the control group.

It should therefore be emphasized that the results of the larger series, including all participating centres, will be required to assess differences in the rarer outcomes such as caesarean section rates and maternal, foetal and neonatal morbidity.

Acknowledgements

PGE$_2$ in triacetin gel (Prepidil gel) was generously provided by the Upjohn Company in the context of the European multi-centre trial monitored by Dr M. Noah (Upjohn Co., Kalamazoo) and Dr J. M. Decoster (Upjohn International, Brussels). We are indebted to Ms H. Wittenberg for excellent help with the collection and analysis of the data.

References

Bishop, E. H. (1964). Pelvic scoring for elective induction. *Obstetrics and Gynecology* **24**, 266.

Calder, A. A. (1979). The management of the unripe cervix. In *Human parturition* (Eds M. J. N. C. Keirse, A. B. M. Anderson and J. Bennebroek Gravenhorst). Leiden University Press, The Hague. p. 201.

Ellwood, D. A. and Anderson, A. B. M. (1981). *The cervix in pregnancy and labour*. Churchill Livingstone, Edinburgh.

Floberg, J., Allen, J., Belfrage, P., Bygdeman, M. and Ulmsten, U. (1983). Experience with an industrially manufactured gel PGE$_2$ for cervical priming. *Archives of Gynecology* **233**, 225.

Golbus, M. S. and Creasy, R. K. (1977). Uterine priming with prostaglandin E$_2$ prior to elective induction with oxytocin. *Prostaglandins* **14**, 577.

Grant, A. and Chalmers, I. (1981). Register of controlled trials in perinatal medicine. *Lancet* **1**, 100.

Grant, A. and Chalmers, I. (1985). Epidemiology in obstetrics and gynaecology — some research strategies for investigating aetiology and assessing the effects of clinical practice. In *Scientific basis of obstetrics and gynaecology* (Ed R. R. Macdonald). Churchill Livingstone, London (in press).

MacKenzie, I. Z. (1981). Clinical studies on cervical ripening. In *The cervix in pregnancy and labour* (Eds D. A. Ellwood and A. B. M. Anderson). Churchill Livingstone, Edinburgh, p. 163.

Thiery, M., Decoster, J-M., Parewijck, W., Noah, M. L., Derom, R., Van Kets, H., Defoort, P., Aertsens, W., Debruyne, G., De Geest, K. and Vandekerckhove, F. (1984). Endocervical prostaglandin E$_2$ gel for preinduction cervical softening. *Prostaglandins* **27**, 429.

Weiss, R. R., Tejani, N., Israeli, I., Evans, M. I., Bhakthavathsalan, A. and Mann, L. I.
(1975). Priming of the uterine cervix with oral prostaglandin E_2 in the term
multigravida. *Obstetrics and Gynecology* **46**, 181.

Discussion

Dr MacKenzie commented that these results differed from those of Ulmsten, whose studies
did not demonstrate side-effects or pain. The difference was presumably due to the fact that
in the study Dr Keirse had presented some prostaglandins had gone directly into the uterus.

Dr Keirse agreed. Some patients had needed analgesia and had required monitoring all night.
One might start at 4.00 a.m. so as not to spend all night on the evaluation, but follow-up was
also necessary, particularly in those cases with medical reasons for induction.

Dr Murray drew attention to 1 patient who had meconium. One tended to forget that if labour
were induced without rupturing membranes then an important clinical sign was lost, emphasizing
the increased importance of cardiotocographic monitoring.

Dr MacKenzie, in conclusion, said that the results of the triacetin gel study were very
encouraging and he hoped that an appropriate preparation might be available for general use
in the not too distant future. He felt that the Meeting had been very worthwhile, and it only
remained for him to offer thanks to Brian Godman for his initial idea in convening the meeting,
the Upjohn Company for their support, Clive Wood who was largely responsible for the
organization, and the Royal Society of Medicine for their hospitality. Final thanks, on behalf
of himself and Dr Calder, went to the Panellists for their most valuable contributions.